Victorian
DETAILS

Victorian
DETAILS

Decorating Tips &
Easy-to-Make Projects

Caroll Louise Shreeve

Sterling Publishing Co., Inc. New York
A Sterling/Chapelle Book

Chapelle, Ltd.
P.O. Box 9252, Ogden, UT 84409
(801) 621-2777 • (801) 621-2788 Fax
e-mail: chapelle@chapelleltd.com
Web site: www.chapelleltd.com

Library of Congress Cataloging-in-Publication Data

Shreeve, Caroll McKanna, 1942-
    Victorian details: decorating tips & easy-to-make projects
Caroll Louise Shreeve.
        p. cm.
    "A Sterling/Chapelle Book."
    Includes index.
    ISBN 1-4027-0922-6
    1. Handicraft. 2. Decoration and ornament--Victorian style. I. Title.

TT157.S527 2006
745.5--dc22   2005024729

10 9 8 7 6 5 4 3 2

Published by Sterling Publishing Co., Inc.
387 Park Avenue South, New York, NY 10016
©2006 by Caroll Louise Shreeve
Distributed in Canada by Sterling Publishing
⅝ Canadian Manda Group, 165 Dufferin Street
Toronto, Ontario, Canada M6K 3H6
Distributed in the United Kingdom by GMC Distribution Services,
Castle Place, 166 High Street, Lewes, East Sussex,
England BN7 1XU
Distributed in Australia by Capricorn Link (Australia) Pty. Ltd.
P.O. Box 704, Windsor, NSW 2756, Australia
Printed in China
All Rights Reserved

Sterling ISBN-13: 978-1-4027-0922-7
        ISBN-10: 1-4027-0922-6

For information about custom editions, special sales, premium and corporate purchases, please contact Sterling Sales Department at 800-805-5489 or specialsales@sterlingpub.com.

Contents

Introduction

My delight in the romance of the Victorian era springs from dress-up experiences in my grandmother Louisa Jane's parlor. There was displayed a variety of fascinating objects and family memorabilia: sepia-toned photographs of relatives in ornate silver frames atop the piano; a massive family Bible sitting ponderously on the library table; the genuine black bear rug, glass eyes gleaming and mouth frozen in a timeless snarl, lying before the fireplace. The bear was shot by my grandfather, or so I was told.

Before Grandma's tall mirror, I tried on her flower-covered, wide-brimmed hats and high-buttoned shoes, which I always needed help closing with a button hook. Then I waltzed into the parlor trailing skirts many sizes too big and stepped back in time. This book allows us to return for decorating inspiration to this era in my grandmother's parlor, when attention to detail was celebrated.

Victorian sensibility delights in lifestyle, and the decorating treatments to support it have often been referred to as overdone and overstated. Nothing could be further from the truth. The highest value of the period from 1837 to 1890, when Queen Victoria envisioned and expanded the British Empire, was mandated as "nothing should ever be done half way." This philosophy went beyond accumulating wealth and power. It went beyond the adage of don't begin if you don't intend to do your best. Doing anything only half way was seemingly incomprehensible.

From the beginning of her reign, the 18-year-old Queen was committed to country, family, and God. Of course, as Queen she expected everyone else to follow her taste for rules, manners, and rituals. Victoria's penchant for taking everything to the extreme is legendary, and specific examples of that sensibility are downright awe inspiring: piano legs, to highlight a particular practice, had to be covered with drapery or fringe, so intense were her beliefs in discrete decorum.

OPPOSITE

A framed print of Queen Victoria with a child beside her is quite at home for a decorative arrangement with tartan plaid vase, sewing box, and pincushion. One of the royal residence of Britain's reigning sovereign is Balmoral on the River Dee in Scotland, so tartan plaids with strong colors of many clans are in evidence in Victorian decorating.

ABOVE

My grandparents posed for this photograph on the occasion of their wedding day in Ohio, thought to have been in 1910. Louisa Jane Miller designed and fashioned her Victorian wedding dress, which my daughter Kimbra inherited and treasures as a keepsake.

Her husband and consort, Albert of Saxe-Coburg-Gotha (an area of Eastern Germany), was the epitome of style. Possessed of flawless manners, Albert lent his name to the Prince Albert coat and introduced to Britain the German holiday tradition of decorating Christmas trees. Yet it was as the creator of the first World Exposition in London that Victoria's companion truly demonstrated amazing skill. His gargantuan glass hall with tree-lined display spaces astonished the known world and presented beautiful art, creative machinery, and the best of what each participating country had to offer. The trend of celebrating the finest in quality and creativity at global gatherings continues to this day. No other famous couple, Victorian or otherwise, can compare to Victoria and Albert.

In the United States, a far more adventurous culture, Victoriana evolved with its own signature during the same period. In architecture, interior design, and rituals of manners, the affluent and middle-class Americans developed their own expressions and knowledge of Victorian taste. Not having a resident aristocracy to emulate, they simply assumed the role! The Industrial Revolution in Europe and the United States meant the middle-class people could at last afford "the niceties." Materialism could finally occupy a similar place as it did for the European aristocracy.

ABOVE

The scale of the glass London Exposition hall amazed visitors who were dwarfed by its trees, sculptures, and vast array of industrial machinery.

RIGHT

My Great Uncle Clarence Hunsaker, grandmother's brother, was proud of his stylish appearance and reputation as "a sport" who loved good cigars, betting on fast horses, and winning good poker hands. I thrilled to his exciting adventures with Indians on the railroad. He was especially proud of his Prince Albert-style topcoat.

Certainly the antithesis of Victorian sensibilities, today's passion for the industrial simplicity of naked steel or simple concrete would not have met with Queen Victoria's intricate tastes. Yet such styles are simply mirrors of one another: "uncover it" verses "cover it up!" And either way, taken to the extreme.

For the Queen's taste, bare bones should never be exposed. Fortunately, there is a great deal of pleasure in selecting interpretations from the rich decorating heritage her era produced on both sides of the Atlantic.

Victorian-style exteriors begin with creative architecture, featuring excesses in surprise and cover-ups with gingerbread fretwork and wrought-iron embellishments. These are the "hard lace" of a home's exterior.

ABOVE, UPPER RIGHT, and LOWER RIGHT
The three photos on this page feature Victorian details that were applied to the exteriors of homes. The elaborate details such as the ornate carvings on the structure of the home, the picket fence, and fanciful painted surfaces transport these homes back in time, as in my scrapbook.

OPPOSITE

Typical of the Victorian's fascination with symmetrical design and scientific displays of exotic butterflies, this side table is appropriately "dressed" in a lace-embellished table scarf, accompanied by fresh flowers and framed family portraits. This arrangement would speak volumes about family social station, moral values, cultural studies of "the botanicals and entomology," and the social grace of a proper cup of tea.

LEFT

Notice how the basic tones of taupe unify the wicker furniture, the figured rug, and the tapestry pillow on this porch.

Indoors, each Victorian space and object receives an elegant enhancement. Layers of lace cover-ups, drapes of luxurious fabrics, and nuances of beauty either capture the light softly or sparkle at every turn. Lavish imports from the former colonies treat the world to the exotic botanicals and arts of India, Africa, and Australia. Sculptures, souvenir travel items, and finely woven fabrics establish themes for sensual home environments. Safari treasures embellish many a man's imposing library. An essence of mystery and adventure pervades the Victorian home, while subtle lighting invites the spirit of romance.

Exotic color influences from Asia, Africa, and the Orient—when Britannia ruled much of the known world—brought the jewel tones of ruby, garnet, cinnabar, and claret into high fashion in the Crown Colonies and America.

Typical of Victorian decorating is dark wood cornices and transoms. An arc of art glass is handsomely set off with a claret and ivory ball-fringed ivory swag roped with tassels. A typical two-toned, late nineteenth-century wall treatment on either side of the centered sideboard features a patterned wallpaper in smoky gray, a textured wooden dado on the lower wall, a matching cornice above, and a painted ivory ceiling visually lowered to the cornice. The ornate gilt-wood rococo mirror is suspended in a tipped-out fashion to reflect more light onto the banquet table. In the Victorian era, two layers of linen and lace tablecloths would be removed after early dinner courses to feature the polished wood surface for dessert, coffee, and perhaps liquor.

Symmetrical arrangements abound in Victorian decorating. A mirror centered between identically matted and framed scenes; a dramatic vase of flowers centered on the sideboard between hurricane candleholders, the swag treatment peaked at the center of the windows and transom, a glass candelabra centered on the table, all would provide the look for a formal dining room.

RIGHT
High-style architecture and appointments are exemplified in this formal dining room from the symmetrical arrangements to the slab of marble draped with lace and placed atop the steam-heat unit, serving as another sideboard.

Perhaps your goal will be to make particular spaces seem a half world away—a dark corner of the empire. Is this a nineteenth-century sitting room in Bombay or Cairo? Maybe it is a governor's home in Fiji or the Solomon Islands.

Regardless of location, the uniting themes for all Victorian-style socializing areas are dark woods and lush heavy fabrics; muted light and ivory-colored, reflective ceiling areas; highly decorative detail on furniture and table coverings, carpets, and picture frames.

Celebrate the Victorian-style details that you can replicate in your own public and private spaces. Within the pages of this book are elegant enhancement projects: country-house-style ideas using fantastic natural materials; elegant manor-style Victorian rooms literally dripping with beads, velvets, ribbons, and fringe. Others are more restrained, with a focus on shape and texture.

Even if you don't live day to day in charming echoes of a Victorian past, you can still enjoy Victorian style during the holiday season. Use our inspirational cues from the country homes of lords and ladies and indulge in decorating with the sublime extravagance typical of royal apartments and castles. Emulate traditional buffets and sit-down banquets with sumptuous table treatments. Dazzle loved ones with bejeweled and beribboned gifts. Treat your holiday guests to the joyful abundance of nothing done half way at your house this year. Let inspiration from *Victorian Details* help you express your delight in the best of decorating, entertaining, and gift giving. In your home, you are the Queen or Prince Consort. Your taste prevails.

With the exception of a few stepped-out directives, most projects contained herein are treated as suggestions. The special techniques required for the novice to accomplish tasks can best be found in the Resource List on page 141.

LEFT
This gracious drawing room welcomes with a Turkish carpet on a hardwood floor, an off-season bank of ferns on the hearth, and richly textured appointments. The heavily carved mantel mirror and fireplace surround make an elegant focal point for this conversation grouping of damask and petit-point upholstered furniture.

CHAPTER ONE

Victorian Bliss

For rich complexity of design in a vibrant dance between intensity and nuance, the Victorians can scarcely be surpassed. Ideals of beauty expressed by their architects and landscaping visionaries inspire replication—restyled—by today's imaginative home and garden designers.

Victorian dwelling designs and construction details were imbued with layers of meaning. Their penchant for elaborate organization and ornamentation created artful and exaggerated styles, which evolved in landscape planning and exterior features.

That wealth of resource detail and an underexplored aspect of amusing Victorian sensibilities can be incorporated into our own landscaping and exterior detail plans. For all their rules—about proportion and scale, social class differences, appropriateness, subject matter from Medieval and Gothic Revival to Far Eastern influences—we must never forget that Victorians also loved to have fun! Their exterior and garden embellishments and entertaining rituals sparkled with lighthearted and even humorous details.

How can you achieve the same effects in your own garden? While personal style will vary far and wide, it is still possible to act Victorian by paying attention to detail. The opportunities in this regard are endless.

The number of color manipulations you can achieve in your selection of plants and flowers is almost inexhaustible. However, you will also want to accent your plant life by selecting ornaments and hidden gems that guests might happen upon during a stroll: statuary, decorative stones, cast-bronze or cast-cement pieces, boweries, and gazebos.

LEFT
This whimsical gazebo with decorative gingerbread fretwork details is the essence of all things Victorian.

Garden Glimpses

Garden ornaments—terra-cotta entablatures with swags of flowers, cooing doves or fallow deer, elaborately figured chimney remnants—can be mounted on a wall or simply leaned against a fence to create period interest today. Wrought-iron lightning rods as well as intricate and amusing hammered-metal weather vanes can crown your roof or a patio post. Cast-cement replicas of cows, sheep, and peacocks can prance through your garden beds, replacing the live ones that browsed Victorian estates.

In Victorian times, guests arrived in horse-drawn carriages and caught glimpses of statues and grazing animals through the hedges along winding entries. Tall hedges, pruned archways, tree groupings, and statuary were designed to create enticing glimpses of such peaceful scenes along the way to the house. It is amazing to note that such "domestic" scenes, as they were known, were often composed to precisely interpret the imaginary landscapes of famous British and French romantic painters of the day. Some commissioned gardeners imported particular trees and plants from a hemisphere away to replicate paintings Victorian patrons knew well. No expense nor effort was spared for these dramatic enticements. They set a mood of anticipation that we still find inspiring.

Wall fountains in the shape of faces or theatrical masks are fantastic finds for the entryway or garden. Many such designs are being reproduced in resin and cast cement at reasonable prices for outdoor display.

To re-create such Victorian garden scenes today, place cast-stone and resin reproductions, actual demolition remnants of heavily figured wood carvings containing birds, roses, and animals around your garden path. Use portions of pilasters, pillars, or columns with classically carved capitals as

ABOVE
Glimpses of a statue, a stone bench, a fountain, or an urn full of flowers were carefully contrived to be enjoyed from many vantage points as one strolled through a Victorian garden.

plinths to hold flower-filled urns and statuary in the contemporary garden or along the driveway. Entablatures as well as wrought- and cast-iron gates, spike-finial fence sections, cast-iron horse-tethering posts, tall iron lantern stands, wall-hung lanterns, and stepping stones also can become much-admired Victorian details.

♛ P R O J E C T

Mosaic Garden Stepping Stone

Take a step back into the Victorian era by creating a stepping stone for the garden. Begin this project with a premade stepping stone or create a shape of your own design, using a mold. Gather broken plates and tile pieces to create a mosaic that is personal and long-lasting.

Materials

- 12"-diameter concrete stepping stone
- Cement-based grout
- Grout sealer
- Heavy-duty construction adhesive
- Tesserae:
  china plates
  stained glass
  tiny tiles
- Wheel glass cutter/nipper

Instructions

1. Cut and arrange glass, plate, and tile pieces in an appealing design on the stone.

2. When pleased with the arrangement, lift each piece, "butter" it with adhesive, and set in place on the stone.

3. Allow to set for 24 hours.

4. Apply grout according to manufacturer's directions.

5. Seal the grout and the stone.

Note: For options, tips, and other imaginative projects for home and garden, using mosaic techniques, refer to the Resource List on page 141.

Topiary Fun

In the terraced courtyards of affluent Victorian residences, clipped yew-hedge topiary designs were borrowed from the fantasy gardens of the previous generations. Twisted corkscrews, elephants, waist-high chess pieces on checkerboards of patterned grass and colored gravel, and miniature battlements were trained and trimmed over wire armatures to the delight of garden strollers.

Today, we can purchase animal topiaries in pots from some nurseries, florists, or catalogs. It is also a reasonably simple process to create your own topiary designs from moss-covered florist foam, ivy trained around a chicken-wire armature, or a more authentic version of training and pruning yew or boxwood plants into shapes for patio or porch conversation pieces. From simple orb shapes to fanciful rabbits, consider the fun of such whimsy as a means of introducing another aspect of gardening to the children in your family or neighborhood. Disney designers capitalized on this idea with living green Mickey Mouse and other fantasy animal forms at theme park entrances to Cinderella's castle in the United States and Europe.

Topiary forms created by florists make a sophisticated statement not only in gardens and courtyards but in an entryway, on a mantel, or as a buffet table centerpiece. Create your own potted topiary from Styrofoam covered with boxwood, moss, or dried rosebuds.

p.s.

This distinctive design can be replicated by purchasing Styrofoam or floral-foam shapes, assembled with or without a rod armature secured to a base with florist tape. Stud the shape with greens and accent with decorative metallic wire strung with faux gem beads and charms.

Victorian Attention to Detail

© Caroll Louise Shreeve

We can take our cues from the Victorians' mixture of whimsical fantasy and serious interpretation of detail. Many roofs were studded with symmetrically arranged dormer windows. Elevated entrances might have paired towers or oriels—bumped-out wall structures several stories high, containing small-paned windows at every level in an exaggeration of the modest bay windows seen in contemporary homes. Extending up to roof level, these were crowned with balustrades and lacy Gothic stonework. Simpler Tudor manor homes, constructed in timber and stucco, were sometimes "faced" with courses of brick in intricate patterns of contrasting color known as polychrome. Imagine what delights could sprout visually from landscapes and rooflines highlighted with a few select Victorian antiques or reproductions.

The one abiding aesthetic rule back then was that all exterior building treatments be perfectly meshed with the style design elements of their complementary garden landscapes, as well as the interior decor. No detail was to detract or seem out of place in the classical-to-casual scheme uniting the entire property. Whether of ornamented or minimalist taste, today's designers agree with the Victorians on this if on no other point.

There exists a rich repertoire of Victorian elements from which to choose in echoing any style from this multifaceted period. Basic architectural styles varied from classical Greek or Roman to romantic and sometimes frowned-upon "pagan" Italian Renaissance. However, traditional Georgian tastes were favored from the 1850s through the early 1900s. Established royal and mercantile families, for the most part, remained wedded to classical styles until the late-Victorian countertechnology of Arts & Crafts designs caught on.

All of these styles merged gracefully from elevated views to their meticulously maintained surrounding grounds receding from the home in terraced levels. Sweeping manicured lawns and meadows—planned for viewing "picturesque" deer, cattle and sheep from the terraces and windows of the house—were punctuated with woodlands in every direction. They featured well-pruned trees, shrubs, rose and rhododendron arbors, and styled flower beds reached by means of stone staircases. Carefully selected details of these landscapes are great fun to replicate in our own gardens.

OPPOSITE
This cast-iron bench becomes a stunning garden focal point with the addition of a gingerbread-arch surround.

ABOVE
Silhouetted against the sky from afar, a Victorian estate whispered its beauty, using spires, turrets, balustrades, tall chimney stacks, cupolas, and sloping roofs of patterned slate. Outer walls of brick might be patterned in geometric polychrome designs. A glass conservatory for exotic plants and tropical entertaining might be set apart from the house, as in the sketch.

Welcoming Details

Victorian castles, particularly royal residences and the manor homes of wealthy industrialists, impressed visitors with tree-lined allée approaches. These graceful driveways leading to multistoried homes inspire landscaped entries even today. Echoes of Victorian circular drives, with multitoned stones arranged in precise patterns, are a trend even as do-it-yourself home improvement projects.

Often boasting a family crest, fence and gate reproductions of Victorian designs continue to be popular with custom builders and may even be acquired, as they once were during the Industrial Revolution, through mail-order catalogs. Replicating Victorian design elements for dramatic large-property entrances, small courtyards, and gated communities has made the use of iron gates and fences today almost as prevalent as in the past.

A welcoming idea in Queen Victoria's time can be created today with equal flair but much less fuss. Enhance an entrance by decorating its perimeter with baskets brimming with flowers. Color-coordinate them with some aspect of the home or its mood. Baskets accenting the sweep of such an impressive entrance were woven of wicker, cast in stone, or crafted in delicate wrought-iron tracery with elaborate scrolled handles.

Regardless of what methods you use, the goal is to frame the entrance to your estate, regardless of size. The point is not necessarily to establish your dominion; rather, you want to convey a sense of welcoming generosity and repose to those who enter. You want your guests to feel comfortable and relaxed. Create the idea that they have entered another world.

OPPOSITE
This impressive cast-bronze urn and plinth were originally erected on the Steinway estate in New York.

ABOVE
The Smith property in New York City recalls the beauty of wrought- and cast-iron enhancements so typical of Victorian landscape structures.

p.s.

Unless planning for short-term special events where wicker can withstand a few days in the weather, arrange flower plantings in weather-proof baskets of cast-stone, cast-cement, bronze, or iron that can remain outdoors all season or even year-round.

To create inviting outdoor spaces, Victorians used classical elements such as symmetrical pillars, porch posts, and carved-stone pedestals to support a basket of flowers or container of ferns. These elements beg visitors to pause for a leisurely cup of tea. Use an ottoman for a tea table. Simply embellish it with beautiful handwork of the Victorian era, such as cross-stitch or needlepoint.

Found in thrift and antique shops, estate sales, and on the Internet, original ottomans are in great demand among collectors and designers. Reproductions of plinths are available for decorative use on porches and can be arranged along entry walks and graduated up stairway risers to welcome guests. The focus is to heighten the anticipation of guests for the delights that await them inside the house and on the yet unseen surrounding grounds. Creating a sense of expectation fairly guarantees your guests a wonderful time.

This porch seating arrangement encourages conversation in comfort on a space defined by a Turkish carpet and armfuls of plump pillows on a wicker settee. A linen-draped ottoman serves as a tea table.

Natural—or alluding to nature—never meant "plain" to a Victorian homeowner, at least not until the Arts & Crafts period in the late 1800s. An early passion for re-creating grottoes with adornments studded with seashells, sparkling quartz fragments, and fake gems made some Victorian nature walks a bit like an *Alice in Wonderland* experience. Similar effects can be captured today, using mosaic garden stepping stones and decorative flowerpots.

Other outdoor surprises ranged from simple rills—very narrow straight or winding stone waterways only several inches wide—to cascading waterfalls, spouting fountains, and numerous ponds and lakes. For Victorians, bodies of water had to be serene and peaceful enough to reflect a statue, a gazebo, or a summerhouse.

RIGHT
This garden chair becomes a display space for a basket filled with cascading plants.

BELOW
This bench, surrounded by a wall of leaves, is used to display flowers as well as provide a quiet spot to relax.

Victorian Porches & Garden Rooms

White painted furniture is as popular today as it was during Victorian times, particularly wicker pieces with bent and curlicue design elements.

The more stately Victorian homes boasted an "exotic" conservatory, or glass addition, which housed Victorian botanical enthusiasts' collections of imported tropicals from around the globe and alpine plants from the Orient. These humid rooms could be of the cold or the hothouse variety, with the latter often incorporating a sitting-room furniture grouping for casual dining and entertaining. The conversations during wintry afternoon teatime must have been delightful amidst trickling fountains and banana and citrus-fruit trees in gigantic pots, while snow drifted down outside. Is that not indeed romantic? No wonder the "sunroom" has regained its stature on the priority wish lists of today's homeowners.

ABOVE
This sunny garden room welcomes conversation amid exotic palms and fresh flowers. The glass walls blend indoors and outdoors into a pleasing place to relax, just as Victorian conservatories did.

ABOVE
This Victorian porch supports the ambience of the garden's living flowers with floral fabric cushions and embroidered lace floral table coverings.

More-modest country homes, in perhaps pitched-roof Queen Anne style, featured porches and verandas in front and often in back as well. Symmetrical stairs led up to balustrade-style railings, the elaborate wooden "lace" of gingerbread fretwork, and graceful pillars that supported a roof, dreamy with climbing roses. The beauty and fragrance of the blossoms were trained to drape in sweetness those seated in shaded wicker settees below.

In good weather, Victorian porches served as gathering places and ideal spots for reflection or high tea. An afternoon reading on the porch was no extravagance, to be sure. A symbiosis existed between the porch as a place to ponder and the garden, which Victorians felt was a source of inspiration.

One can imagine smartly appointed ladies and gentlemen of the era seated on a spacious open porch, discussing the news of the day over tea and biscuits. Beyond the railing, nature went about its business in service of Victorian ideals.

UPPER RIGHT

A small table with a drawer for napkin rings, silver flatware, and linen napkins could as easily keep secret a private journal or a stash of elegant stationery for an afternoon's correspondence.

LOWER RIGHT

Fluted columns, cast-iron openwork railings with an Eastern arabesque influence, and a practical painted floor form a perfect backdrop for a charming porch tea or brunch. Turned spindles and carved crests on the backs of a pair of wooden chairs are further graced with needlepoint seats.

CHAPTER TWO

The Victorian Language of Flowers

Flowers symbolized to Victorians love, romance, civilized living, and impeccable manners. The human connection to what nature/God provided as beauty and nourishment was developed in ordered monastery gardens over hundreds of years. Wars, military ranks, Biblical references, family crests, monograms, and house names revolved around the importance of the rose and the lily in particular. Religious art was filled with the symbolic significance of flowers. Employing flowers as message bearers was practiced as much out of habit from medieval times as Victorian ideals of romance. Indeed, medieval and Gothic influences permeated Victorian culture in both spiritual and practical matters. Period novels, by such authors as Jane Austen, have many garden scenes and contain meaningful exchanges of flowers between tortured or blissful characters.

The supreme order of all things botanical—from the most delicate of mosses to an imposing stand of oaks on a terraced knoll—absorbed the interest of Victorians. They categorized, imported for study, and hybridized plants from the farthest reaches of the globe. This fascination with flowers—and by extension butterflies, bees, exotic insects, birds—was celebrated in textiles, porcelain, silver, and even wrought- and cast-iron relief. Victorian artisans and manufacturers created graceful floral items as both decorations and gifts, and these creations inspire us still to decorate with nature's magnificence.

A gentleman caller might express his meanings to his lady with a bouquet of Anemone (anticipation), Tulip (declaration of love), Honeysuckle (devoted love), or Nutmeg Geranium (expected meeting). He would wait anxiously for her floral response. It might range from one single Rosebud (confession of love), a single teasing nosegay of Dandelion, Day Lily or Morning Glory (coquetry), Lavender (distrust), Yellow Carnation (disdain) to Michaelmas Daisy (farewell). The exchanges of flowers and letters might continue for many months or social seasons before culminating in marriage or despair.

Nature's Flowers
Set the Mood

FAR LEFT
Symmetrically arranged vases of flowers set a formal mood, especially when contained in silver and accompanied by a collection of porcelain objects. Notice how the colors in the floral bouquets echo the flower colors in the porcelain tableware.

LEFT
An intimate bouquet of vibrant lilies and snapdragons acquires extra charm from an elaborately decorated vase with gold-leafed handles.

Symmetry as found in nature's flowers, insects, and birds satisfied the Victorian penchant for order in its most elegant forms. Nature's symmetry was borrowed to bring the garden indoors year-round. It's not surprising that daily Victorian life incorporated endless allusions to floral forms, colors, and fragrances. Capturing and displaying "pinned" insects, as well as pressed blossoms, ferns, and herbs, was a popular pastime of the day. The framed art and albums that resulted became vital topics if conversation lagged at table or tea.

Fresh flowers cut for arranging indoors ranged in size from tiny nosegays to towering arrangements suitable for a grand buffet, an entry hall table, or a prominent mantelpiece. A bedside table might only be large enough for a book and an intimate vase of heady roses, but the importance of freshening rooms, particularly for guests, was a gracious touch no hostess in Victorian times would omit. Rose or lavender water was steeped in the kitchen to sprinkle on dainty handkerchiefs and personal as well as household linens. Flowers and their essences permeated Victorian life.

Important Victorian social functions took their dramatic cues from the architectural details and exquisite nuances of nature's flowers. The blossom and foliage colors might be powerful or subtle, but an abundance of them massed for fragrance and style made an unmistakably opulent statement. Guests would feel honored at the effort and expense put forth for their personal benefit.

Such are the joys we can share with friends and loved ones in our own entertaining. Using floral designs to set a mood of gracious hospitality makes guests feel particularly welcome and appreciated.

Arrangements of fresh, pressed, and dried flowers set the mood for a room, a season, and a specific occasion. Floral choices reflect the passages of life: births, christenings, coming-out balls, engagements, weddings, anniversaries, funerals. Gay holiday flowers particularly appropriate to each event can be given and displayed. Victorian gardens were cultivated to support just these occasions, as well as the herb and vegetable needs of the kitchen.

OPPOSITE
Victorian dining rooms gave their hostesses a grand stage on which to present commanding floral arrangements. Mantels, sideboards, and buffet tables proved the perfect pedestals.

ABOVE
An antique milk-bottle caddy full of original glass containers makes a showy and surprising means of massing pink roses for a contemporary interpretation with Victorian spirit.

p.s.
A silver or porcelain tray of glassware in concert as vases in a group would be equally lovely.

Floral Images in Abundance

From parlor to boudoir, flowers blossomed in hand-wrought items as well as fresh-from-the-garden displays. Foliage, flowers, and fruits such as lemons, pineapples, pears, and grapes were the subject matter of all Victorian decorative arts. Needlework, tole painting on wood and tin household items, china painting on tea service plates, beadwork, and floral-embossed silver and porcelain were universal.

Transferware processes made these items available to the middle class, for whom the expense of commissioning hand-painted items was prohibitive. Floral upholstery fabrics and tapestries, silk and satin flowers, draperies, stenciling on furniture and plastered walls, wallpapers, and clothing were created by hand and by increasingly mechanized factory operations. These original items and reproductions are in great demand by decorating enthusiasts and collectors.

p.s.

To create romantic Victorian luxury in the bedroom, coordinate chintz or damask roses from window treatments to pillows, bed linens, flouncing skirts, and wall art.

OPPOSITE
In this room, the delightful touch of a convex mirror suspended in a window reflects to perfection all floral details.

UPPER RIGHT
This table featuring cherished family photographs is relieved with fresh seasonal flowers placed in a porcelain pitcher.

LOWER RIGHT
The lace garlands of silk flowers woven through the canopy enhance the floral abundance used in the Victorian era.

Faux Fireplace from Vintage Bureau Top

This mirror support for a late Victorian Eastlake bureau was found in a consignment shop. It seemed perfect as the surround for a faux fireplace, incorporating the brass heat vent on the wall in my bedroom. Woodworkers located three polished granite windowsills from the demolition of a Victorian-era hospital. We used them for mantel and hearth. Faux marbling on Bondo™ provided believable width to the mantelpiece.

The chimney shelf was constructed from the inverted piece removed from the bureau's mirror support base. A template from the "fireplace" design elements was used to create the shelf supports. A plate rail was cut into the shelf top; then the surround, hearth frame, and shelf were spray-painted with textured stone paint.

Materials

- 1½"-wide wood pieces (2 for each end and 1 for full length of mantel back)
- Bondo™
- Bureau mirror support
- Drill/drill bit
- Gold antique leafing pen
- Hand saw
- Masking tape
- Paintbrushes
- Paints:
  black
  desired shade, deeper than room's wall color
  faux granite to match mantel
  textured stone
  white
- Pencil
- Polyurethane
- Recycled polished granite windowsills (3) *Note: 2" x 6" wooden planks to appropriate lengths and faux-paint to resemble marble or granite can be used instead of recycled granite windowsills.*

- Sandpaper
- Screws
- Tack cloth
- Tracing paper
- Woodworking tools

Instructions

1. Remove hardware. Sand, brush, then wipe with tack cloth all carved and varnished surfaces of bureau mirror support.

2. Saw bottom horizontal wood piece free. Save to create faux chimney shelf.

3. Spray front of mirror support with textured-stone paint. Allow to dry overnight.

4. Using woodworking tools, cut and assemble additional wood to back the transformed bureau top and fireplace facing. Extend granite mantel with 1½" wood pieces on both ends and along full length of mantel back to fit wall. Attach with Bondo.

5. Faux-paint mantel extensions to match granite, then paint with three coats of polyurethane.

6. Miter three strips of wood to hold hearth slabs, drill holes, screw into floor. Mask and spray with textured-stone paint.

7. Paint inside of the fireplace with a deeper shade than the room's walls; white for trim, edged with gold antique leafing pen; and black paint just inside fireplace surround to resemble marble or onyx. Seal with polyurethane.

8. For chimney shelf, create cornice supports by making a template from fireplace elements. Cut plate rail in bureau component. Assemble. Spray with textured paint to match fireplace.

p.s.

The furnace sends heat pouring out of this "fireplace" for cheery winter nostalgia. I hang Christmas stockings from the mantel for the holidays and set a pot of ferns on the stone hearth for the summer.

Victorians borrowed liberally from natural patterns and textures in choosing decorative details. Flower designs became the adornment of choice for everything from reading chairs to area rugs, with upholstered furniture bridging the gap and footstools in between.

Decorative flower designs were fashioned on boxes and books, using pastel ribbon, and pottery was selected specifically as a coordination of natural elements in one area or another of a particular room. Simply set some floral-patterned bowls and pitchers on stacks of books or little boxes to vary the heights within the arrangement for more interest.

OPPOSITE

Between symmetrically arranged pairs of lamps in two sizes, is centered a small vase of flowers used to bridge the space between the smaller lamps. The ruffled chair anchors the loops of swags above the window and embraces the circular pattern of the area rug. The dainty upholstered bench serves as a table.

UPPER RIGHT

Garden floral details can be combined in a corner focal point such as this to include a lamp base made from a floral-patterned pitcher grouped with a larger collection. Vertical styling on the wall for framed floral and insect art with flower-decorated platters carries the eye upward to embrace a floor-to-ceiling arrangement.

LOWER RIGHT

Delicate enhancements such as the ribbon embroidery shown on this album cover were well loved by Victorian needlework enthusiasts.

CHAPTER THREE

Color It Victorian

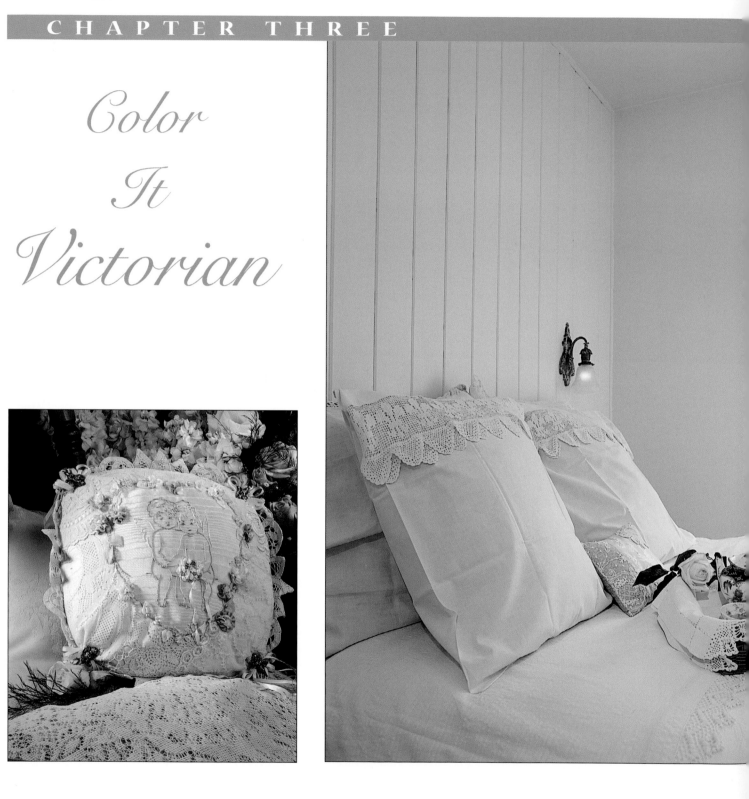

Distinctive Victorian color styles range from simple understated country hues to elaborate "Royal Treatment" rich colors of robust jewels. The epitome of rich styling is found in the Victorian Christmas colors ruby red, gold, cobalt blue, and emerald green, celebrated in the final chapter of this book.

Victorian-era hues were influenced by Britannia's exotic colonies in Africa, India, the Orient, and the Indies, as well as the royal houses of France and Bavaria. Whether layered in white lace or draped in velvets and tapestries, Victorian domestic surroundings comforted all that entered. Simple tips for creating an ambience of grace and refinement are best understood by exploring a few of the better-known Victorian color families.

White-on-white Details

White on white is deceptively sensual. Cool, detoxifying, white gathers quiet energy. It is clean and strong. Create white space in your home. There are as many tints of white as the mind and technical capability can imagine.

Embroidery threads and linen weaves, for example, come in crisp bright whites, eggshell, ecru, and all ranges in between. Exposure to light and moisture, handling, washing, pressing, and the thread counts of needlework applications, all play a part in the apparent whiteness of textiles. Antique linen, cotton, silk, satin, and other fibrous materials have ranges of white all their own.

It isn't necessary to precisely match whites and creams in order to decorate with them. What makes such keepsakes special to the contemporary eye is their personality, the implication of how they were used and enjoyed by women who appreciated beautiful items many generations ago.

p.s.

Add heirloom interest to your home using ethereal tints of ivory and textures from satiny smooth to peeling paint rough.

White has many sister associations for women of the Western world. We think of the pure clean white of delicate snowflakes, and of wispy clouds in a heavenly sky. White lilies, snowy tulips, and creamy roses bespeak nature's purity and fill rooms with heady fragrance and the perfection of elegant form. Each reminds us of a higher more inspiring nature than is obvious at first glance.

Wedding veils and gowns, christening gowns, formal white gloves, gossamer lace edges on bed linens and lingerie, luminous pearls, all capture the spirit of pristine beauty and value. White snow and white lilies, by example, embody fleeting beauty. White Carrara marble, from stone quarries in Italy, was a prized material in the classical era for use in timeless urns, statuary, and building components; it remains so today.

White on white is a color scheme that can handle a great many delicate details without appearing overly busy. The all-white palette allows the eye to flow uninterrupted throughout a space and can enlarge the effect of a small room.

In Victorian times, milk glass and ceramic glazes on pottery and porcelain—intended to emulate the iridescence of pearl—were valued according to their clay-body and glaze translucence and their embossed treatments. Politically incorrect today, Victorian ivory carvings, piano keys, and incised keepsakes were treasured for their pale radiance. They remain collectible today even as they patina to golden shades with age.

White can be visualized as mounds of delicately peaked meringue on an enticing coconut cream pie, or spirals and dollops of whipped cream swirled into steaming cups of hot chocolate. A taste of "white," as in white chocolate, frothy eggnog, or divinity candy, is a feast for the tongue or the eyes—an ambrosia of the moment to be treasured.

LEFT

The white furniture and billowing white sheers of this sunroom evoke the fresh air and sweet breezes of the out-of-doors. The woven textures of wicker and textile add interest, along with green plants, to a room that might otherwise feel medicinally austere.

Of course, the cleanliness of white surfaces is hard to maintain. So Victorian servants scoured marble with a paste of vinegar and salt, whitened cotton and linen with bluing agents, and bleached rust marks from a lady's or gentleman's bathtub.

Ever-practical English and American Victorian-era country homes employed simple kitchens and larders, white ironstone china, cotton and linen-trimmed bedrooms, white painted furniture, and hand- or machine-made lace accents. Today's shabby-chic recalls the comfort and unrestrained beauty of that period's carved-wood furniture ornamentations and the linens gently worn in daily living.

Our hearts are warmed by such elegant details from the past. Living closely with them slows down the hectic present and recalls an era when time was not such a hot commodity. Aristocratic people, who had great quantities of time, performed activities such as a bit of handwork or pressing correspondence to fill the hours meaningfully, lest time be wasted sitting by the fire. White on white is a decorating palette that appears elegantly effortless.

p.s.

In your busy world, dedicate at least one corner of a room you'd like to make more restful to a pleasing arrangement of white and cream objects. Arrange them in a painted cupboard or on a table layered with textured ivory linens.

White Rose Pillows

The elegant white-on-white appearance does not necessarily require different shades. You can achieve the same effect using texture.

Choosing slightly different shades of white for the fabric and crochet thread, respectively, in these pillows is certainly an option. However, notice that the texture and pattern of the crochet casts shadows that become different hues on their own. Simply link trefoils of leaves and large roses with chain stitches for a beautiful set of white-on-white boudoir pillows.

Materials

- 9"-square gauge
- 45"-wide white fabric (9 yds)
- Polyester stuffing
- Size 10 steel crochet hook
- Size 10 white crochet thread 250-yard balls (3)
- Thread to match

Instructions

Note: For additional instructions on crocheting, refer to Resource List on page 141.

Finished sizes not including ruffle: large pillow: 20" square; small pillow: 20" x 10"

Rose motif (make six): Ch 8, join with a sl st to form a ring.

Rnd 1: Ch 1, 24 sc in ring, sl st to first sc.

Rnd 2: (Ch 4, sk 3 sc, sc in next sc) six times, sl st to base of beg ch.

Rnd 3: Work (sc, dc, 3 tr, dc, sc) in each ch-4 lp around, sl st to first sc—six petals.

Rnd 4: Holding petals to front of work, *ch 5, sc from back of work in next sc bet petals, rep from * around, sl st to first sc.

Rnd 5: Work (sc, dc, 3 tr, dc, sc) in each ch-5 lp around, sl st to first sc.

Rnd 6: *Ch 7, sl st in center st of next petal, ch 7, sl st in st bet next two petals, rep from * around, sl st to base of beg ch.

Rnd 7: Sl st to center st of next ch-7 lp, *ch 7, sl st in center st of next ch-7 lp, rep from * around, sl st to base of beg ch.

Rnd 8: Work 7 sc in each ch-7 lp around, sl st to first sc.

Rnd 9: Ch 1, sc in each of 7 sc, *(ch 3, sl st in third ch from hook to make a picot) twice, sce in each of next 14 sc, rep from * around, sl st to first sc.

Rnd 10: (Ch 20, sk 7 sc, two picots, and 6 sc, sl st in next sc) six times, sl st to base of beg ch.

Rnd 11: Work (sc, 24 tr, sc) in each ch-20 sp around, sl st to first sc.

Rnd 12: *(Sc in each of next 5 sts, picot) four times, sc in each of next 5 sts, rep from * around, sl st to first sc. Fasten off.

Large leaf (make 72): Ch 12, sc in third ch from hook, sc in each ch to last ch, 3 sc in last ch, working back along opposite side of ch, sc in each ch to end, turn. *Ch 2, working in bk lps only, sc in each st to center sc at base of leaf, 3 sc in next st, sc in each st to last st, sk last st, rep from * five times more for seven points on leaf. Fasten off.

Small leaf (make 24): Ch 14, sc in third ch from hook, sc in each ch to last ch, 3 sc in last ch, working back along opposite side of ch, sc in each ch to end, turn. *Ch 2, working in bk lps only, sc in each st to center sc at base of leaf, 3 sc in next st, sc in each st to last st, sk last st, rep from * three times more for five points on leaf.

Joining: Whipstitch three large leaves tog at base to make a trefoil for corner of square. See photograph on page 49. Make four trefoils for each square.

Position rose motif in center, a trefoil in each corner with center leaf pointing away from rose motif, and four small leaves bet trefoils with tips pointing clockwise around square. See photograph. *Note: Be certain to keep ch from twisting while joining pieces.*

Join thread with sl st in tip of a small leaf, *ch 4, sl st in tip of next large leaf, ch 13, sl st in second picot of adjacent scallop on rose motif, ch 10, sl st in shortest point on side of same large leaf, ch 10 sl st in third picot on same scallop on rose motif, ch 10, sl st in shortest point on side of next large leaf, ch 10, sl st in last picot on same scallop of rose motif, ch 15, sl st in tip of same large leaf, ch 4, sl st in base of next small leaf, ch 10, sl st in second picot on adjacent rose motif, ch 10, sl st in next picot on same scallop of rose motif, ch 10, sl st in tip of same small leaf, rep from * around as established, end with sl st to base of beg ch.

Rep for rem five squares.

Assembly: Large pillow is four blocks square. Small pillow is two blocks long. Tack tips of center leaves of trefoils tog to join blocks

Finishing: *Note: Use ½" seam allowance.* Cut fabric for front and back of both pillows before cutting bias strips.

Large pillow: Cut two 21" squares from fabric for front and back. For ruffle, cut 11"-wide bias strips, piecing as needed, to measure twelve yards. Cut strip into two equal lengths. Fold one strip in half lengthwise with right sides facing. Stitch both narrow ends. Turn and press. Stitch gathering threads along raw edges through both layers. Divide strip into fourths and mark. Pin strip to right side of pillow front, aligning raw edges and placing marks at corners. Gather to fit. Stitch. Repeat for remaining strip. Place pillow back over front, with right sides facing and ruffles toward center. Stitch around three sides, making sure not to catch ruffles in seam. Turn. Stuff firmly. Turn under seam allowance and sl st opening closed. Tack crocheted piece right side up on pillow front.

Small pillow: Cut two 21" x 11" pieces from fabric for front and back. For ruffle, cut 7"-wide bias strips, piecing as needed, to measure eight yards. Cut in half and finish strips as for Large Pillow above. Mark center of each edge of pillow front. Pin strip to right side of pillow front, aligning raw edges and marks. Finish pillow.

p.s.

Try creating a practice swatch of the crochet pattern you will be using before starting the actual project. Compare this swatch to the gauge presented by the pattern. If the swatch does not match, readjust the gauge until it matches, then start the project.

White with One Color

With crisp white linens and white paint as a background canvas, adding one additional color creates harmonious, simple beauty. Innumerable Victorian original keepsakes and reproductions can revive the period to your particular taste. Consider Wedgwood bone china or jasper decorative display pieces in blue/white, gray/white, or brown/white. Transferware pottery in blue/white or brown/white is another subtle approach to the simplicity of white with a single color. Peach/white, and sage or putty green with white, are soft color combinations that combine seamlessly for a pleasing palette.

For wall or floor colors, any of the aforementioned hues in a pastel tint can be used to cover large areas, and can be continued in a more intense shade through accent items. This limited color approach to decorating unifies a room or an entire home, providing solidity of design that holds together items of various sizes and patterns.

Red-and-white Turkeywork embroidery and transferware, as well as black-and-white Victorian parquet floors, are other one-color-with-white themes to emulate. Blue and white—the ultimate sky, clouds, water combination—has been favored for centuries in the Orient and is celebrated in English and American china coupled with the Victorian love of flower, bird, and butterfly images.

UPPER RIGHT
This collection of blue-and-white transferware placed in an antique white hutch creates understated drama in an all-white kitchen.

LOWER RIGHT
The red motif of this transferware adds one touch of color to this white room.

English country style is always memorable and restorative in blue and white; it's a restful color combination. Kitchens, bedrooms, and baths are particularly suited to blue-and-white decorative treatments—imagine a single lemon in a blue-and-white bowl. The power of a small punctuating accent in a gentle two-color room is delicious. Consider this combination for any room where water is an element and relaxing is the emotional focus.

Remember that pairing a single color with white is a technique that enables you to use shades of that color, not just a single hue alone. A range from cobalt to sky blue on white gives a room much-appreciated diversity, and still meets with Victorian standards.

p.s.

White ruffles and lace work well with one colorful pattern for competition.

OPPOSITE

Who says white with one other color implies the use of solids only? This rose-hued floral pattern on walls and ceiling embraces the white canopied bed like a bowery. Each window's balloon valance blossoms with a fabric that matches the wallpaper.

UPPER RIGHT

Vertical pink stripes alternating with flowered stripes at the window bring a simple white room cheery elegance. The quilt folded on the end of the bed brings the pastel tints into the room. It emphasizes the white-painted iron bed and its brass top rail and finials. Shelves suspended from the ceiling repeat the bed frame's strong horizontals.

LOWER RIGHT

Tints of red on the antique coffeepot complement the red transferware dishes and light fixture while providing some bright color to this white dining room.

A hardy sideboard of aged wood makes a stunning backdrop for a collection of blue-and-white transferware and willow or pottery. Arranged symmetrically with paired and centered items, white with one color—blue in this case—is very typically Victorian, particularly in a country setting.

While coordinating a bed or bath with white and one color is a relatively straightforward design task, doing the same in the kitchen is a challenge. Consider dividing the kitchen into separate nooks or spaces in which to apply white and one color. Don't use too many—you don't want it to look like a rainbow.

OPPOSITE

Transferware pottery with matching linens is a great embellishment to a hutch, kitchen, or pantry shelves.

ABOVE

Arrange a collection of porcelain tea caddy and serving pieces and teatime will take on a romantic significance well worth a pause in one's busy day. Set up a similar vignette of favored blue-and-white items on a side table, a tray, or in "pride of place" on the mantel.

UPPER RIGHT

The use of white with blue accents on the tile, dishes, and light fixtures creates a calming effect in an otherwise hectic room. The turned furniture legs and decorative plates add to the overall Victorian feeling of this kitchen.

LOWER RIGHT

The coordinating color china items add to the beauty of practical cabinet organization.

Exotic Victorian Gem Colors

There is no question but that the acquisition of colonies during Queen Victoria's reign had an immense effect on the lifestyle of affluent Victorians in London and America. The thriving merchant trade brought not only exotic objects and categories of unknown plant life to the curious, but luxurious new colors and textures as decorative elements. Cinnabar, cobalt, and ruby dyes, and fabrics enriched with pearl, ebony, gold, and silver, were much sought after. Throughout the entertaining and private areas of the Victorian home, textiles with these rich qualities of design and craftsmanship were prominent.

The library where gentlemen sat sipping brandy and smoking imported cigars after dinner featured walls lined with brown and burgundy leather-bound volumes, many embossed with gold. The paneling was sometimes accented by stuffed hunting trophies. On the floor would have been elaborately patterned Eastern carpets woven from the finest wools and dyed in the richest reds and blues anyone had ever seen. Fabrics and carpets the color of aged red wine were enhanced by woven images of flowers, birds, and animals as well as graceful twisting vines on the borders.

Cigars were preserved in a humidor of some exotic and inlaid wood. Carved-horn ornaments, animal skins and furs, cut velvets, and heavy damask throws dripping with fringe and tassels decorated these rooms reminiscent of the palaces of biblical kings.

p.s.

Scatter golden berry branches and ruby candles to recall the Victorian passion for exotic inspiration from China, Persia, and Africa.

OPPOSITE

The robust hues of early autumn flowers burst with vibrant life barely contained by a transferware pitcher. The Eastern influence of combining purple, red, orange, and gold is apparent in such a bouquet.

ABOVE

The dark woodwork in this master bedroom enhances the rich colors used in the bedding and floor rug. The heavy-looking curtains accented with tassels create an exotic look yet the room still retains its Victorian feel.

The Victorian parlor or drawing room, even the occasional bedroom where ladies received visitors and entertained, was generally lighter in feel and temperament concerning theme, color, and texture. Chinese and Japanese embroidered silks and hand-painted or transferware porcelains were popular additions to a lady's tearoom, whether in the main house or in a glass conservatory.

The smoking of small dark, imported cigarettes was a decadent pleasure in which some upper-class women indulged. Fancy containers for the cigarettes, as well as "breath freshening" snuff boxes, were the female counterparts to the gentleman's cigar box.

Privacy was a primal need to a Victorian, particularly a lady. Sumptuous master suites, often adjoining, were draped with tapestries, velvets, brocades, layers of lace, tassels, furs, and fringes. Often his dressing and sleeping rooms were heavier in feel and color than her more feminine suite. Both areas exhibited Bombay chests and lacquered furniture.

OPPOSITE

The closets in this top-floor sitting room are American Victorian since the British had fewer closets. The beauty of the alcove is enhanced by crocheted faux-gingerbread fretwork.

RIGHT

Peach, pink, rose, and gold fabrics create this "haremesque" effect, expressed in layers streaming from an elaborate rococo cornice. The ruffled sheers are gathered on pocket rods behind the cornice and a glitz of brass is repeated in the cornice above the bed.

p.s.

Rich reds, deep blues, and celadon greens are ideal tones for mixing florals, stripes, and "crazy quilt"-style textiles.

Ribbon Sachet

A lavishly feminine heart sachet is ideal suspended from a curtain tieback or swag, hung from an armoire knob, or given as a fragrant gift to a loved one. This sachet is both an example of and a slight deviation from the Victorian practice of decorating with hues of a single color. Notice that the ribbon woven together to create the heart-shaped body of the sachet centers around a dusty rose color, but individual strands of ribbon deviate to either side of the color continuum. Included are paler tints of pink, but also light grays, pale blues, and even beige and purple. The key is to not choose colors that deviate dramatically from the central color scheme. The effect is like looking through a child's kaleidoscope.

Materials

- ⅛"-wide silk ribbons:
  beige (1⅛ yds)
  brown (1⅛ yds)
  dk. pink (1⅛ yds)
  dusty rose (1⅛ yds)
  gray (1⅛ yds)
  lavender (1⅛ yds)
  pink (1⅛ yds)
  purple (1⅛ yds)
  tan (1⅛ yds)
- ¼"-wide silk ribbons:
  pink (5")
  tan (5")
- 1"-wide pink silk ribbon (6")
- 4"-wide cream lace scrap or doily
- 5" x 6" dusty rose print fabric for back
- 5" x 6" muslin
- Antique jewelry piece
- Assorted cream buttons (8)
- Brass charms (2)
- Copier paper
- Fabric glue
- Needles
- Pearls (6)
- Pencil
- Polyester stuffing
- Potpourri as desired
- Scissors:
  craft
  sewing
- Small gold metallic braid (5")
- Thread to match
- Trims:
  ⅛"-wide cream picot (⅜ yd)
  ¼"-wide cream picot (½ yd)
  ⅜"-wide cream lace (½ yd)
  ½"-wide decorative (½ yd)

Instructions

1. Trace Ribbon Sachet Pattern on page 138 onto copier paper. For woven ribbon heart, cut four 5" lengths and three 6½" lengths each from ⅛"-wide beige, brown, dusty rose, gray, lavender, pink, purple, and tan ribbons. Trace heart on right side of woven ribbons. Sew ⅜"-wide cream lace with design toward center of heart.

2. With wrong sides facing, stitch woven piece to back on marking, leaving an opening. Repeat, stitching ⅛" outside first row. Trim to 1/16" around outside row of stitches; press. Stuff with polyester and potpourri. Stitch opening closed.

3. Glue ½"-wide trim on back edge, mitering at point. Fold braid in half. Tie knot 1" from fold for hanger. Glue ends to heart front cleavage. Cover heart front with lace scrap as desired; glue edges. Weave pink ⅛"-wide silk ribbon through ¼"-wide picot trim. Align edges of woven trim on back; glue. Loop and glue ⅛"-wide picot trim to heart front as desired, anchoring trim with five pearls.

4. Stitch running thread on one long edge of 1"-wide pink ribbon; gather to 1½". Glue to heart front cleavage. Glue jewelry to ribbon with charms and buttons on either side; see photo. Make a gathered circle with ¼"-wide ribbons, gluing to heart front at point. Glue remaining pearl to center of gathered circle.

Extraordinary lacquered furniture imports were the height of fashion in Victorian parlors, drawing rooms, and a lady's or gentleman's private quarters.

While the craftsmanship and design of these pieces were impressive and reliable (so many pieces still exist today), they were initially noticeable for their color and flair. In essence, Victorian furniture pieces served as artistic palettes around which a room or section of a room could be decorated.

Wall colorings, carpet designs and individual decorative elements were chosen according to coordination with colors in an elegant piece of furniture. While today we might pick a sofa that goes with carpet and paint, in that era just the reverse was practiced.

p.s.

To emulate this look in your home, include Arabian and Persian medallion imagery—the Victorian's delight—as grounding in the carpet pattern. Other Eastern influences appear in the suspended cane light fixture, reminiscent of Byzantine palaces.

UPPER LEFT
This unique scroll-armed settee with a woven-cane back sets a romantic mood for a lady's leisurely pursuits. A monogrammed workbox for writing or needlework rests upon an ottoman with needlepoint upholstery, serving as a conversation table.

LOWER LEFT
Notice the decorative touch of a luxurious fringed tassel hanging from the drawer knob. The tapestry throw, red roses, and green grapes enhance this opulent corner arrangement, which centers on the elaborate decorative painting on the cabinet, framed by a peach wall.

Victorian dining and drawing rooms established family position and style for members of the home, servants, and guests. Chandeliers sparkled over dark burnished-wood tables glittering with lead crystal glassware and white bone china. Meals and high teas were served on sparkling silver trays amid polite conversation. Paintings of important family members stared down from elaborate gold-leafed frames on mahogany paneled walls.

Sconces for candles, and later gas lights, cast a warm glow in a room rich with the colors of precious gems: ruby red, emerald green, sapphire blue. Family crests and monograms expressed a tone of formal dignity on crisp white linens, radiant silver, and delicate dinnerware. Flowers of red, gold, purple, and white—coordinated to match existing decor—graced buffets, tea tables, and sideboards. Protocols existed for everything, which gratefully we can ignore.

Victorians on both sides of the Atlantic perfected color-coordinated groupings of furniture and decor conducive to leisurely communication. The same option is available to us today. Use dominant furniture pieces to convey a rich, dark weathered elegance. Use an off-white rug to create a subtle contrast. Introduce splashes of bright color through flowers, both fresh and dried, placed on tables around the room. The usage of subdued lighting will help create a tranquil mood.

BELOW

In this contemporary Victorian dining room, blue, brown, and gold accents repeated in the curtain and the wall and hutch displays stand out against a white background. The monogrammed chairs add a subtle statement to the richness of this room.

CHAPTER FOUR

Artfully Displayed Collectibles

Victorian decorating develops from owners with a vision for fitting small, delicious collection pieces into impressive period interiors, giving massive furniture a delicate touch. In this, the longest chapter in the book, we explore the seven basic themes most commonly pursued and displayed by vintage collection enthusiasts.

If Victorians were obsessive-compulsive about anything, it was the organization of every detail in their individual worlds, especially their collections. Cabinetmakers designed custom file cabinets and credenzas; collectors cabinets with numerous drawers and subdivided shelves; elegant secretaries that often had secret compartments; elaborate shipping trunks for personal wardrobe garments, shoes, and jewelry items; chiffonier storage cabinets, and more.

These pieces of finely crafted furniture are in great demand by antique collectors, as are collectible theme items. Reproductions are available of many such pieces and they can be incorporated beautifully into contemporary decorating schemes, though individual decorators may give furniture and containers surprising practical uses. What could be more whimsically Victorian than a wooden sheet-music "vitrine" or newspaper "canterbury" holding a collection of needlework patterns or favorite magazine issues?

The Writing Arts

Elegant correspondence, calling cards, and invitations were requirements bespeaking the social graces of the Victorian era. No less significant today, courteous correspondence can incorporate personal qualities such as embossed stationery and handwritten RSVPs, thank-yous, and notes of condolence. These personal efforts still send a message of sincere attention to detail with Victorian spirit.

Among the popular collectibles for library and desk displays are inkwells, fountain pens, feather quills, wax sealing tools, sand shakers, decorative letter openers, antique stamps, stamp-decorated items, vintage postcards, Victorian stationery, personal and business calling cards, place cards, and engraved invitations. Fortunate are the collectors who can acquire these simple and elegant necessities of proper Victorian correspondence.

Family held highest priority in Victorian society. Gatherings of family images in exquisite frames of many sizes and shapes were arranged in small spaces. Albums featuring family members and significant life events were popular for handing around at teas and social visits.

These much cherished items were often kept in the writing desk, where a Victorian lady would spend a great deal of her day corresponding with cherished friends and family.

Of course, she would have been well-versed in the art of calligraphy, which is certainly also an option for us today. Free or low-cost calligraphy classes are frequently offered at local community or art centers. Not only will your close friends and acquaintances appreciate receiving a handwritten note, they will also be immeasurably impressed with your skill.

p.s.

Replicate this delightful custom by scanning and printing your own family photos in sepia tones or black and white, then display prominently in a collection of vintage frames.

OPPOSITE
A collection of crystal and art-glass ink stands and inkwells with embossed silver lids graces a polished wooden secretary.

UPPER RIGHT
In this vignette, a variety of embossed metals, inlaid wood, tortoiseshell, silver, and ceramic items harmonize beautifully with shared shapes, colors, and designs.

ABOVE
Small silver frames and pedestal vases, antique address books, and calling-card albums add an authentic Victorian romance to the grouping.

Framed vignettes of memorabilia and travel souvenirs from grand tours were a hallmark of the Victorian period. A portable box for needlework or writing was an essential traveling companion for Victorian ladies—and with regard to correspondence, for many gentlemen as well. A Bohemian studio desk or writing corner was not complete without a collection of keepsakes and framed family portraits.

To show off your collection, layer an arrangement of them with a jewel-handled magnifier and inkwells on a small desk or table. Accent with satin roses and change the display seasonally to incorporate Victorian valentines, Christmas and Easter cards, and correspondence. If you do not have any of your own Victorian keepsakes, they can be purchased at thrift and antique shops.

OPPOSITE
Victorian greeting cards, inkwells, and enameled stamps are artfully displayed on this small desk, adding a sense of casualness and warmth to a room.

UPPER RIGHT
Here, the tiny opera glasses repeat the collectibles idea of the framed personal memorabilia displayed above.

LOWER RIGHT
The miniature hinged hands featured here were designed to hold calling cards, invitations, and pressing thank-yous. Notice how the dried pansy wreath echoes the round display tray and marries the square box to the other items.

Lacy Basket Card

Delight a friend with an elegant greeting card personally crafted by you. While it has become an axiom that handcrafted gifts carry more meaning, the statement has not lost its powers of truth.

This is not a time-consuming project, but it will be evident to a friend or family member that you took the time to make it yourself. The benefits are obvious to all involved. The recipient gets to feel particularly prized and cared for. You get to experience another's joy at truly being valued, and you get the satisfaction of creating with your own hands—an added bonus.

Materials

- ¾"-wide lavender wire-edged ribbon (¾ yd)
- 7" x 10" drawing paper
- 12"-square lace-like paper napkin
- Craft scissors
- Dried small flowers:
  purple
  violet
- Paintbrush
- Pencil
- Tacky glue
- Tiny purple/blue glass beads (25)
- Tracing paper
- Watercolor paints:
  blue
  purple

p.s.

To make a gift set of note or greeting cards, create one beautiful handmade card. Using a color photocopier; copy as many full-color images as desired. Using a spray adhesive, trim and mount each color copy on a prepared cardstock card. Three-dimensional embellishments also photocopy beautifully.

Instructions

1. Fold drawing paper in half, aligning short ends. Paint front of card blue. Let paint dry.

2. Cut corner of paper napkin to make triangle measuring 7" on longest edge. Working with fold at top, glue triangle with point facing down onto front of blue card.

3. Draw desired pattern for basket onto tracing paper. Cut out. Paint basket purple. Let paint dry. Center basket on napkin triangle.

4. Glue purple and violet flowers to top of painted basket. Tie ribbon into bow. Glue ribbon to card. Glue beads to card as shown in photograph above.

Victorian Bookends

These decorative and practical bookends give a Victorian flair to your desk or writing shelf. Of course, you want to choose a location to display the bookends where they will get noticed by guests. The top of a desk is a fairly obvious place. If they are used on bookshelves, make certain at least one is placed prominently on the end if a shelf.

Materials

- Fabric marking pencil
- Fabric scissors
- Glues:
  craft
  industrial-strength
- Matching pair of brown metal bookends
- Matching pair of wooden wall frames
- Needle
- Picture or photograph
- Ribbon roses (2) purchased or made from ½"-wide rose silk ribbon *Note: See Step 6.*
- Thread to match
- Wire-edged ribbons:
  brown/dusty peach ombré (66")
  ivory sheer (52")

Instructions

Note: For instructions on ribbonwork refer to Resource List on page 141.

1. Insert picture into each decorative wooden wall frame. Using industrial-strength glue, adhere wall frames to metal bookends. Let glue dry.

2. Using fabric scissors, cut ombré ribbon into two 26½" lengths. Mark each length with four 5" and one 6½" intervals. Using a loose running stitch, gather one long edge of one length and pull to marked points, securing in layered petal fashion, allowing longest length for outermost petal. Repeat for remaining ribbon length.

3. Fold each flower in half and glue together with craft glue. Glue one flower to top center of each wooden frame.

4. Cut ombré wire-edged ribbon into two equal lengths. Coil and stitch each length into a circular ruffle. Pucker with fingers as desired.

5. Glue one circular ruffle to center of each large flower.

6. Glue one purchased or handmade ribbon rose to center of each circular ruffle. To make a ribbon rose, gather-stitch one long edge and roll ½"-wide silk ribbon into a bud. Secure with stitches as tightly as desired.

7. Cut ivory wire-edged ribbon into two equal lengths. With one length, tie bow that is 5½" wide with 7" tails, making a four-loop bow. Gather-stitch down center of each looped bow. Tightly gather and secure thread. Repeat for second length.

8. Glue one bow behind large flower at center back of each bookend. Glue ribbon tails to side of bookends and shape bow loops and tails as desired.

The Needle Arts

Victorian ladies and young girls prided themselves on achieving perfection in the needle arts. For practical, cultural, and spiritual reasons, creating beauty with needle and thread was expected in most classes of society in Victorian Britain and America. I recall learning, before I was six years old, the proper tension on my crochet thread for making window-shade pulls over bone circles. Grandma was definitely of the old Victorian school.

During my childhood, Grandma was in her seventies and eighties. I remember her teaching me to darn my own socks on a small smooth gourd, and to create leaf and petal shapes and French knots on linen with colorful embroidery threads. Of course, first I had to master counting threads on bleached flour or sugar sacks. I knitted scarves with yarn scraps, crocheted doilies and rag rugs for my doll's house, strung beads on buttonhole thread pulled through a bar of bee's wax, and made hand-edged buttonholes. What I "must learn to do" was lovingly drilled into me so that I could grow up and "amount to anything." Whichever needle art was taught me, nothing less than perfect would do or it had to be done over.

OPPOSITE

Vintage linen guest and tea towels are collectible for both their charming motifs and their precise and imaginative handwork. Here, displayed in folded and layered fashion, are child-themed linens. Images of embroidered whimsical animals and children, along with framed sepia-toned portraits of children and miniature toys, make an adorable focal point for a little one's guest room.

UPPER RIGHT

This vintage jelly jar of antique buttons, with a ladle, encourages the curious to sift endlessly through the tiny textured treasures.

Sewing, knitting, crocheting, and tatted-lace making were activities I observed and participated in when Grandma filled the parlor with her church "Lady's Aid" friends. Many arrived for meetings with tapestry bags or fancy boxes that held embroidery materials and hoops, knitting yarns and needles, fancy or simple thimbles, and pretty handmade pincushions with tiny scissors attached. I entertained myself for hours, sorting buttons of tortoiseshell, mother-of-pearl, jet, ivory, and Bakelite at their feet, listening to plans for the war effort or talk of fashion in ladies magazines. I "kept still" and held out for Grandma's berry pie and a cup of honey-sweetened tea. Little did I realize at that young age that these childhood experiences would lead me to collect handmade items later in life, or even to incorporate buttons and fibers into my scrapbooking layouts.

Collecting vintage needle-art tools and finely crafted antique items is an irresistible obsession for anyone who appreciates purposeful, timeworn beauty and is inspired by all things Victorian.

With the Victorian passion for organization and control, an effort was made to counter the social upheaval resulting from the Industrial Revolution. In every area of life, systems of order were embraced. The affluent could afford custom cabinetry in which to organize household linens for both ordinary and special occasions. These cabinets were also where the family's petticoats, monogrammed handkerchiefs, kid gloves, silk hosiery, and so forth were kept.

Whether hand-embroidered or machine-produced, monograms and family crests hearken back to letters from medieval manuscripts. The combination of embroidered monograms and symbolic motifs created family stories that Victorians appreciated hearing.

In the modern era, we can call these monograms and crests a worthwhile pretense. While the Age of Kings may officially be fading, there is no reason to abandon the era of lords and ladies. After all, it's the beauty and cultured living we pursue, not the dominion. Family crests and monogrammed pieces demonstrate a pride in family and willingness to embrace that immediate community.

OPPOSITE
This custom cabinetry has a special place for each item. The cabinetry is not only used to store items but is the room's main decoration.

UPPER LEFT
The sheaves of wheat with the uncial letter D and the flower basket entwining the Old English W bespeak the pursuits of their namesakes. A bountiful harvest is expressed in stylized wheat sheaves.

ABOVE
Lace-edged monogrammed linens complement an elegant silver coffee server from one of the late Victorian reform styles. An elongated silhouette of container, handle, and spout are graced by a restrained frieze of flowers at the base of the coffeepot. The silver treatment and the simple embellishment of the linens reflect the new "less is more" sensibility.

Monograms were popularly produced in all of the Victorian needle arts, as here on guest towels. Monograms and family crests are also collectible on silver goblets, serving pieces, and flatware. They spoke eloquently of the importance of family and social position. Practically speaking, when sharing silver at family picnics and other gatherings, sorting gracefully whose was whose at the close of the event was much easier.

Simple embellishments for everyday linens were often stitched by young girls, beginning in their preteen years to fill a "hope chest" dowry of household tea towels, dresser scarves, and guest towels.

p.s.

Hand-embroidered linens can still be found in reasonably good condition at estate sales, thrift shops, and antique shops. If what you want is not available, consider purchasing a vintage kit or consulting a book with patterns and directions for the theme you have in mind.

LEFT

Hand- and machine-embroidered decorative borders are lovely vintage accents for a guest room or bath. Compare the simple Eastlake geometric elements on the towel at upper left to the ornate flower borders and medallion accents on the other examples.

ABOVE

This medallion of pierced "buds" and French-knot blossoms accented with satin-stitched leaves at intervals is typical of a near sampler approach to embroidery-stitch mastery.

OPPOSITE

These antique wedding photographs are accentuated by monogrammed linens and a silver goblet. Peach silk roses add a touch of color to this opulent display.

"Layered" curtain window treatments are typical of Victorian tastes and prevailed in all but the Arts & Crafts Movement beyond the turn of the nineteenth century. The effect created by having both a sheer layer near the glass and heavier curtains partially draping the windows is one of increased privacy and filtered light. Of course, re-creating this Victorian technique is very simple in the modern age. Both opaque curtains and heavy draperies are sold in sizes created to fit most windows.

p.s.

Turn a plaid tablecloth into a charming window swag by cutting and hemming its sides to fit the window width, allowing for a bit of curve to the folds. Purchase the necessary yardage of lace edging for the window width, and a bit beyond as desired. Stitch the lace edge to the width of the tablecloth for the bottom. Fold and stitch a top rod-pocket sleeve or attach painted wooden rings to slip onto a painted wooden rod with turned finials for a vintage effect.

OPPOSITE
This layered white window dressing over white-painted sashes is country-cottage tasteful with Victorian spirit. A corded-tassel tieback allows the lace-edged curtains to transmit light with style. The vertical openwork finishing seam on the sheer curtain was once a hand-stitched technique, but had been replicated on a machine by the 1850s.

UPPER RIGHT
This window swag made from a lace-edged tablecloth adds a charming touch to this kitchen window.

LOWER RIGHT
The sheer panel gathered in the center allows usage of the window, while the valance creates the layered look that mirrors Victorian taste in window treatments.

Old English Blocks

For most Victorian ladies, the goal was to create details in a room that friends would notice almost immediately upon entering. Hardly a ploy, this is the way society functioned. Success could be measured by the number of breathless compliments one received before, during, and after a social gathering.

Inset squares laced with picots combine with linen to drape a parlor table. The picot edging and tassels celebrate Victorian spirit in detail. Imagine this table runner in peach, teal, or lilac with white picot edging as a white-with-one-color alternative.

Materials

- 2½" gauge square
- 17½" x 43½" ecru linen
- Needle
- Size 10 steel crochet hook
- Size 20 ecru crochet thread (6 balls)
- Thread to match

Instructions

Note: For additional instructions on crocheting, refer to Resource List on page 141.

Square (make 16): Ch 20

Row 1: Dc in eighth ch from hook, (ch 2, sk 2 ch, dc in next st) four times. Ch 5, turn.

Rows 2–5: *Sk sp, dc in next dc, ch 2, rep from * across. Ch 5, turn. Fasten off after row.

Rnd 1: Join thread in any corner, ch 1, (3 sc in next sp) twice, *ch 3, sl st in third ch from hook to make a picot, 3 sc in next sp, picot, 3 sc in next sp, ch 14, turn, sc in third sc in next sp, picot, 3 sc in next sp, turn, (3 sc, picot) five times in lp just made, 3 sc in same lp, 7 sc in corner sp, 3 sc in next sp, rep from * around, end last rep with 4 sc in same corner as beg, sl st to first sc.

Rnd 2: Sc in same st, *(ch 10, sk 1 picot, sc in next picot) twice, ch 10, sc in corner st, rep from * around, sl st to first sc.

Rnd 3: Work *(3 sc, picot) three times in next ch-10 lp, 3 sc in same lp, rep from * around, sl st to first sc. Fasten off.

Assembly: Refer to photograph for placement, lay five squares in a row with corner picots touching. Tack picots tog. Join a square bet bottom edges of second, third, and fourth squares of first row. Join another square bet bottom edges of the two squares of previous row.

Rep for 8 rem squares.

Tassels (make 6): For each tassel, cut 48 (6") strands. Fold strands in half. Tie a piece of thread around strands at fold. Tie another piece of thread tightly around strands about 1" below fold. Tack a tassel to center picot on bottom corner of first square, center square, and last square on each end of table runner.

Finishing: Place a crocheted piece on one end of linen with joined picots ½" above bottom edge of fabric. Trace around the top of the squares. *Note: This tracing will look like five triangles.* Remove crocheted piece and cut linen along marked lines for inset. To hem inset, turn under ⅛" twice, clipping seam allowance as necessary. Pin. Rep for opposite end. Continue folding under seam allowance along long edges of linen. Sl st hem and press. Match crocheted piece to inset. Tack picots to fabric. Rep for opposite end of table runner.

Edging: With right side of linen facing and piece turned to work down one long edge, join thread in corner, ch 1, sc in same place, working sts through fabric and over hem, ch 3, sl st in third ch from hood to make a picot, *7 sc, picot, rep from * across fabric edge, end with sc in corner. Fasten off. Rep edging on rem long edge of fabric.

Victorian Sun Catcher

The crystal in the center of this sun catcher will grab people's attention, but the intricate needlework that frames the stone will hold it. The crocheted detail on this remarkable window ornament looks every bit like a sizeable snowflake. The advantage is that it can sit in the window all year long.

Materials

- Size 30 white crochet thread (1 ball)
- Crystal teardrop
- Gauge:
  4 rows dc = 1"
  20 dc = 1"
- Size 8 steel crochet hook

Instructions

Links: Ch 3, dc in first ch, *ch 3, dc bet ch and dc (2 links made). Rep from * until desired number of links are made. Make 48 ch 3, dc, links. Sl st in first link. Join, being careful not to twist.

Rnd 1: Working down the ch 3 side of the links, sl st to center of first link, (ch 6, sc in next link) around, end with sl st in beg ch.

Rnd 2: Ch 6, sc in next lp, *ch 3, hold back the last lp of each dc, work 3 dc in sc just made, thread over, pull through all lps, ch 1, -closure-, hold back the last lp of each dc, work 4 dc in the third ch of next lp, thread over, pull thread through all lps, (ch 4, hold back last lp, work 2 dc in the ch 1 -closure- of first petal, ch 4 sl st in same place) twice, ch 4, holding back last lp work 3 dc in same place, thread over, pull through all lps, sc in next lp, (ch 6, sc in next lp) twice, rep from * around, end with ch 3, dc in beg ch (12 flowers).

Rnd 3: Ch 7, sc in next lp, *ch 7, sc in point of first free petal, ch 7, sc in second free petal, (ch7, sc in next lp) twice, rep from * around, end with ch 4, trc in beg ch.

Rnd 4: (Ch 7, sc in next lp) around, end with ch 4, trc in beg ch.

Rnd 5: Ch 7, sc in next lp, *ch 6, 2 dc in third ch, ch 3, sl st in same place, (ch 3, 2 dc in same place, ch 3, sl st in same place) twice, ch 3, sc in next lp, (ch 7, sc in next lp) three times, rep from * around, end with ch 4, trc in beg ch.

Rnd 6: Ch 7, sc in next lp, *ch 10, sc in center petal of flower, ch 10, sc in next lp, (ch 7, sc in next lp) twice, rep from * around, end with ch 4, trc in beg ch.

Rnd 7: Ch 1, 5 sc in lp just made, (5 sc, ch 3, 5 sc) in next lp. *(5 sc, ch 3, 5 sc, ch 3, 5 sc) in next lp, ch 3, (5 sc, ch 3, 5 sc, ch3, 5 sc) in next lp, (5 sc, ch3, 5 sc in next lp) twice, rep from * around, end with 5 sc, ch3, sl st in beg ch.

Butterfly Center:

Row 1: Leave two center ch links open directly under three-petal flower. Attach thread in next link, ch 9, sl st in fourth ch from hook for picot, ch 10, sl st in fifth ch for picot, ch 9, sl st in fourth ch for picot, ch 5 sk two links, sc in next link, ch 3, sc in next link, turn.

Row 2: Ch 7, work a trc cluster in center picot of last row as follows: thread over hook twice, insert hook in center of picot, thread over, (pull through two lps) twice, hold back last lp of each, work 4 trc in same place, thread over pull through all lps, ch 9, sl st in fourth ch just made for picot, ch 5, work a dc cluster in same picot as before, holding back last lp of 4 dc, thread over and draw through all lps on hook, ch 9, sl st in fourth ch for picot, ch 5, work one more dc cluster in same picot as before, ch (sl st in fourth ch for picot), ch 5, work a trc cluster in same picot as before, ch 7, sc in next link of center, ch 3, turn, sl st in beg ch of first row of butterfly. Fasten off. Starch heavily.

The Glitter of Glass

Victorian glass collectors are by far the most common among all types of collection enthusiasts. Among the favorite pieces sought by this well-populated group are stemware, leaded-glass serving pieces and candlesticks, scent and medicinal bottles, wine and liquor decanters, art-glass fanlights and transoms, beveled glass doors and windows, and elaborate chandeliers.

Arranging glass collections in unique ways is nearly as much fun as gathering them in the first place. As you think of where best to display transparent, translucent, and opaque glass objects, consider where the light will have the greatest visual impact. Light reflecting off surfaces or passing through to display spectrum colors and repeat other colors and textures in proximity enhances their individual beauty. Small glass items can be gathered into groups for more prominence in a decorating scheme. This is especially true of faceted surfaces of teardrop pendants, chunky inkwells and pen holders, elaborately designed scent bottles, and candlesticks.

p.s.

Double the drama by arranging glass objects on top of or in front of a mirror. Combine with fresh flowers or fill with colored water to fashion a focal point on a tabletop or fireplace mantel.

ABOVE

These jardinieres are placed randomly, and the flowers are grouped occasionally. One low all-white bouquet balances the candles, bringing the eye down to connect the overall arrangement with the perfectly balanced, scrollwork details of the fireplace cornice. The arrangement appears deceptively simple, but is every bit as contrived as the rococo design.

OPPOSITE

Complementing the rhythm of the ornate rococo revival mirror and fireplace is an arrangement of transparent glass vases and lidded candy jars. The symmetrical centering and pairings of the tallest finials on the lidded pieces anchor the overall display.

Jellies, pickles, relishes, and mustards were Victorian staples used to enhance ordinary fare with piquant flavors. Serving pieces for each were uniquely crafted to present condiments with flare and complement the color of the designated contents. Cut- and pressed-glass condiment containers in quilt and hobnail patterns remain popular collectibles. Special serving spoons, spearing forks, and miniature ladles are equally delightful to collect and pair with the appropriate glass container, held in a handled caddy for passing around the table.

Of course, the culinary accoutrements are not foreign to us now, but serving them in a particular manner may be. Guests at an upscale barbeque would certainly be impressed by ketchup in a sterling silver container.

 p.s.

Utilizing mirrors and polished silver trays in a reflective manner can give the most modest glass collection incredible presence.

UPPER RIGHT

Transparent bell jars and glass-domed cake stands unite in this gathering of serving pieces. Both flat and pedestal presentations are dust-free, practical, and beautiful. The smaller items are grouped in the center of the arrangement in a shielded triangle, balanced with an apex of tiered sweetmeats and bonbons.

CENTER RIGHT

These exotic elements of bamboo and imported wood from the Far East and tulips from Holland, arranged amid the glitter of a mismatched group of footed glassware, would have delighted a Victorian.

LOWER RIGHT

A mirror, subdued lighting, fragrant roses, and a gallery tray set the stage for boudoir drama. These crystal scent bottles are arranged symmetrically so their ornate stoppers are paired, then reflected above and below for triple the glitter and glow.

OPPOSITE

This collection of intricate art-glass containers in silver caddies creates a stunning and practical display.

Etched-glass Stemware

As we have established, style in Victorian times was a pursuit of individual expression, such as monograms and family crests. Expressing individual style in modern times is decidedly easier. Putting your particular imprint on glass dining items is quite simple, using etching cream and bit of greenery.

Materials

- Craft scissors
- Eye protection
- Glass-etching cream
- Rubber gloves
- Set of wine glasses, plates, or a tray
- Small leaves from bamboo, china doll, fern, or ivy *Note: One leaf is needed for each glass, and three leaves needed for each plate or tray.*
- Small paintbrush

Instructions

Note: This project is not suitable for children. Etching cream can be hazardous. Be certain to follow manufacturer's instructions. Use in a well-ventilated area, use rubber gloves, and wear long sleeves and eye protection.

1. Thoroughly wash and dry glass items.

2. Cut small leaves from plants, and make certain they are dry.

3. Wearing rubber gloves and eye protection, and using paintbrush, coat back side of leaf thickly with etching cream, following manufacturer's instructions.

4. Using end of paintbrush, carefully press entire leaf onto outside of glass surface.

5. Carefully peel leaf from glass. Let cream dry on glass item, following manufacturer's etching instructions.

6. Wash glass thoroughly.

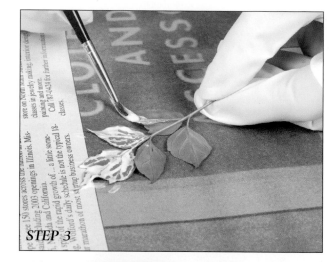

STEP 3

STEP 4

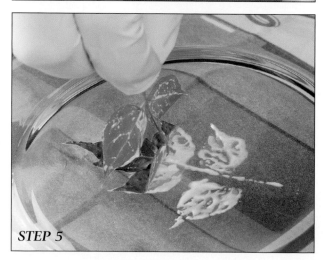

STEP 5

Porcelain Keepsakes

Victorian china can be found in a dizzying array of qualities and styles. Ironstone pottery and transferware are the heaviest ceramic items. Porcelain that is hand-painted or gilded with gold leaf, and bone china made from the finest white kaolin clays are the most precious. If you are fortunate to have inherited or collected these, you indeed have keepsakes to enjoy, display, and pass on as heirlooms to loved ones.

As with glass, experimenting with imaginative ways to display your china is a great deal of fun. The natural marriage of period furniture and antique china in many rooms of your home, or even in the garden, will be reminiscent of Victorian decorating.

Decorating with china pieces becomes more of an artistic pursuit if you see each piece as a small sculpture and utilize it in ways that focus on shape instead of function. In an art gallery, sculpture can be grouped according to style, period, artist, material, or subject. What draws certain pieces together for you? Which pieces would you choose to focus on?

As we've seen on previous pages, symmetrical groupings indicate Victorian influence. But you could also choose asymmetrical arrangements for a modern effect.

UPPER LEFT
Notice how the curved handles of this collection of pitchers are all turned in the same direction to create a frieze-like pattern on a shelf or mantel.

ABOVE
This refreshing display of chains of china plates suspended in cascades on a wall creates a wind-chime effect. The changing shadow play thus created makes this an especially imaginative wall design.

OPPOSITE
A classical corner hutch with sculpted-shell recess at the top, not only acts as the perfect display space for creamy tureens and pitchers but its arc is repeated in the chair backs to unify the elements in this room. The serving pieces are appreciated as curving shapes without the distraction of painted flowers or other transferware imagery.

This display of porcelain and pottery is deliciously Victorian in mood due to a visual focus on curving details. Draped muslin, dresser scarves, and lace doilies drooped in scallops pull together stacks of saucers and plates leaning in rails. Centering a pitcher or plate stack topped with a pudding dish on each shelf solidifies what might otherwise appear tipsy and haphazard. Hand-painted porcelain floral items can be displayed in front of a lady's dressing mirror for double the effect. This kind of tiny vignette is a delightful study in Victorian floral pattern detail.

p.s.

Remember that all of your porcelain pieces need not be a complete set in order to display them. Try shopping in thrift stores and antique stores to obtain unique pieces to mix and match.

OPPOSITE
Notice how the dark cupboard background allows the dishes and lace to have a unifying backdrop in contrast to the white details.

LOWER LEFT
This miniature chest of drawers—each one lined with satin and left open in graduated, stair-step fashion displays quaint hand-painted buttons, knobs, and drawer pulls.

LOWER CENTER
These hand-painted porcelain hat pins and pill and snuff boxes with a floral theme are arranged on a delicate rose-motif plate.

LOWER RIGHT
Adding display punch to a modest collection is this charming glass "sandwich" frame. The delicate lace fragment becomes a miniature stage, holding four tiny hand-painted porcelain containers.

A Bounty of
Boxes & Baskets

As mentioned earlier, Victorians were consummate organizers. Being prepared was defined as the ability to carry organized items from place to place in order to continue a writing or needlework project or to deliver gifts to shut-in loved ones. We can take decorative cues from the Victorians by putting vintage containers to work in fresh new ways, or simply by giving them focal-point status in our collections.

One joy of collecting is learning about myriad and particular uses for vintage items inherited or picked up in second-hand shops. Victorians were ingenious in devising customized items to hold and organize oft-used items.

Adaptations of items from all over the world for uses in the home and garden kept inventors awake at night. Artists in other parts of Europe and the United States were highly influenced by imported items as ordinary as the wrapping paper on imported teas and spices. Lidded, hinged, inlaid, and lacquered items were all the rage in the Gilded Age.

In this modern age, pieces from that era offer both organizational and decorative potential. You will know where to find each little item while simultaneously demonstrating your aesthetic sense.

Of course, it will be important to coordinate your boxes and baskets with other room decor. A delicious lacquered box will not necessarily match country cottage decor, and would feel more at home in a more formal room. Conversely, rustic baskets are right at home in a country setting, but don't mesh well with red velvet and detailed Persian rugs.

OPPOSITE

In humble Victorian country mode, a shabby-chic-style hutch serves as a display cabinet. The pale paint is in soft and homey contrast to the earth-toned textures of the baskets. Notice the rhythm created by the curves and handles.

ABOVE

Lacquerware from the Far East and Africa recalls spice chests brought by caravan to delight Victorians hungry for travel and adventure. The chest allows favored items to peep out from tiny drawers for the whimsical appearance so enjoyed by our Victorian forebears.

Wooden boxes with unique shapes remain irresistible to collectors. Many of the wooden boxes have locks, a remnant of the days when precious imported teas were brought long distances on guarded ships. Tea caddy contents were locked away from servants who might be tempted to borrow a "smidge."

Inlaid marquetry patterns on wooden cigar, stationery, and match "caskets" were often collected by Victorian gentlemen and ladies. If the contents were private or expensive, locks and tiny keys were de rigueur. These boxes, available in many sizes and shapes, are delightful finds in antique shops. Hand-painted or decoupage copies are also popular as collector's items.

When prowling antique stores, look for the various and unusual shapes in which Victorian boxes were made. Perhaps you'll come upon a dark mahogany cylindrical box with light wood inlay; luck might lead you to a rectangular casket with a rounded lid; hidden in a corner might be a truly unique polygon with a gently curving convex lid.

UPPER LEFT
This dainty pier table welcomes guests as a foyer focal point. The oval-framed formal portrait of a child beckons for an arrangement of special small treasures. The simple beauty of this pear-shaped wooden tea caddy is enhanced by its graceful brass keyhole.

LOWER LEFT
These wooden boxes, which feature inlaid marquetry patterns, were used to hold cigars, stationery, or personal items.

Of course, not all the boxes bearing Victorian treasures were made of wood. Small enclosures also had to be crafted for jewelry, and many of these types of boxes could be considered jewels themselves today. While the basic materials with which boxes were crafted changed, the basic elegance remained the same, and all were lined with velvet or satin to protect precious inner cargo.

Consider setting up such a miniature display on a dressing table or a lovely tray. It's easy to see why a superbly crafted box in pristine condition is nearly as important to collectors as the jewelry it was made to protect. Satin- or velvet-lined and leather, velvet, wooden, or silver exteriors make these little boxes treasures, even if their original contents are missing. Other jewelry can be placed inside if you are lucky enough to happen onto these charming boxes.

Just because a collection is only in its beginning stages doesn't mean it can't be made visually more important with a bit of imagination. In other words, don't despair if you only have a box or two. A pretty bracelet, for example, accompanied by a few roses, can anchor a third object to link the items in a harmonious group that appears more cohesive and elegant than two boxes alone.

UPPER LEFT
This footed silver snuffbox, with a lift-out ceramic lining is paired with a green enamel compact in this detail arrangement for a bureau or jewelry cabinet top.

LOWER LEFT
The dramatic black-and-white cartouche-shaped box with its scroll-work feather pin is arranged as the centerpiece in this vignette collection.

Boxes for ladies' lace collars, jewelry, and kid gloves were not only beautiful but they were also practical storage items. Pearl-encrusted collars and delicate handkerchiefs were social necessities when traveling. Many changes of clothing—often several a day—were expected of guests by their hosts.

These lovely boxes and their contents were seen to by servants assigned to care for guests and choose appropriate embellishments for taffeta gowns, silk blouses, and velvet skirts. A gentleman's cravats, cuff links, cummerbunds, and other accessories were housed and transported in equally suitable boxes, handled by the host's butlers.

Even those who couldn't afford servants emulated the wealthy with pasteboard and papier-mâché boxes ordered from catalogs. Some boxes were satin lined for a gentleman's bowler, if not a lady's feathered hat. Their various shapes and were embellished with printed paper celebrating flowers, animals, birds, and festive scenery.

Since no lady or gentleman would leave the house with a bare head, every occasion warranted a hat and a box to keep it in. Happily, today we can replicate as many of these beautiful hatboxes as we like with basic inexpensive products and simple techniques.

p.s.
Decoupage and fabric-covering techniques can render hobby-store boxes beautiful today.

UPPER RIGHT
Fabric-covered boxes were used to hold accessories such as pins and handkerchiefs in a Victorian lady's dressing room.

LOWER RIGHT
A marvelous array of vintage hatboxes makes an enviable decorative statement atop an armoire.

Stylish Victorian Hatbox

You probably don't wear wide-brimmed and/or feathered hats. But that doesn't mean a hatbox that might hold a hat wouldn't add a great deal to your home. After all, the goal here is to look Victorian at home, not necessarily out and about.

This decorative and stylish hatbox provides a discreet storage opportunity of which only privy insiders will be aware. With whom you choose to share that information with is up to you.

Materials

- Fabric scissors
- Hand-sewing needle
- Hot-glue gun/glue sticks
- Octagon hatbox covered with burgundy fabric
- Thread to match
- Wire-edged ribbons:
  1½"-wide burgundy taffeta (2 yds)
  1½"-wide dk. iridescent burgundy taffeta (1 yd)
  2¾"-wide dk. iridescent burgundy taffeta (2½ yds)

Instructions

Note: For instructions on ribbonwork refer to Resource List on page 141.

1. Using fabric scissors, cut burgundy ribbon into nine 8" lengths. Make each ribbon into a twisted rosebud.

2. Using 2¾"-wide dk. burgundy ribbon, mark three 5" lengths, four 7" lengths, and five 9" lengths on ribbon. Gather three 5" intervals for Row 1 into a circle. Stitch petals to hold together. Gather four 7" intervals for Row 2 into a circle. Surround Row 1. Stitch petals to hold together. Gather five 9" intervals for Row 3 into a circle. Surround Row 2. Stitch petals to hold together to complete Rows 1–3 of stitched flower.

3. Hot-glue one twisted rosebud to the center of the stitched flower.

4. Hot-glue stitched flower to top center of box lid as shown in photograph above.

5. Gently swag dk. iridescent burgundy ribbon around side of box lid, twisting ribbon at beginning and end of each swag to hold. Secure with hot glue at center of each panel, and make certain ribbon ends swag together.

6. Hot-glue remaining twisted rosebuds at each twist. Conceal beginning and ending of ribbon under a rosebud.

Polished Silver Accents

Arguably, there is a tendency to view silver pieces for their utility. Oh, they might be decidedly upscale—an indicator of status and success, but still they are often evaluated for what they can do—what purpose they serve.

What of how silver pieces look? What if they are approached as art first and tools second? After all, the number of potential patterns and monograms on pieces of silver is endless, and the way certain pieces are crafted and decorated makes them pieces of art twice over. They become perfect for arranging and enhancing in a variety of settings.

Victorians were masters of the artful vignette, and polished silver played an important role in the creation of those vignettes. A gallery tray not only carried roses and a porcelain tea service, but it also identified the lady of the home's attention to exquisite detail. Her ability to combine the heady fragrances of tea, roses, and pastries with the glint of silver would guarantee high social status.

Based on tradition, polishing silver was the tedious job of servants in Britain's affluent families. This task doesn't appeal to many people with today's hectic lifestyles. Modern young people prefer dishwasher-safe service pieces for dining. They are less than interested in enjoying silver in the bedroom or as decorative items elsewhere in their homes.

For people like myself, polishing silver is therapeutic relaxation. Silver is one of those elegant metals you want to bring off the shelf and use. If you have not inherited silver keepsakes, it isn't difficult to find special pieces at auction, in thrift and consignment shops, and in antique stores. Finding ways to incorporate silver objects into daily life is a challenge worth overcoming. Nothing is quite as elegant and wonderful as love-worn silver.

OPPOSITE
Interlocking embroidered letters of a graceful monogram pair beautifully with the polished glow of scroll, shell, and foliage patterns in this monogrammed flatware.

ABOVE
Notice how the sugar bowl at lower left is not filled with loose sugar nor with sugar cubes, but with sugar lumps. It's also a pleasing surprise to present sugared fruits and flowers in such a manner.

High-style Victorian china and silver service heirlooms are to be treasured. In the British continental manner of eating, elaborate monograms and floral designs also appear on the backs of silver flatware, as food is brought to the mouth neatly on the back of the fork. Of course, monograms exist on the front of each piece as well. When combined with a family crest on each plate and serving piece, the place setting is so lovely as to compete with any culinary delight. Again, polished silver becomes not just the method by which food is served, but also the decorative enhancement of both the table and the cuisine. Set them out in this manner for a buffet brunch or display your silverware collection in a sugar bowl on a sideboard or in a gently lit curio cabinet. Scroll patterns and flowers, beaded edges on rims and bases, and curving handles create a pleasing harmony of distinct yet related details—all playing with light and reflection.

The symmetry of Victorian times would require an entire set of matched silver, each piece sporting a vivid family crest or monogram. As we have seen previously, modern decorating does not dogmatically require symmetrical design. Given the availability of fine monogrammed silver, you could also create a mismatched set that bears a potpourri of emblems and markers. Of course, you must still make every effort to coordinate the set, even while it contrasts. Don't choose incompatible styles or clashing designs.

OPPOSITE
A classical silver urn and matching pieces reflect the beauty of the rose petals and creamy porcelain, while the feet of the gallery tray and sugar bowl echo the urn's footed base.

UPPER RIGHT
Elaborate monograms and floral designs are revealed on the backs of silver flatware as well.

LOWER RIGHT
Mismatched silver handles bloom bouquet style from a diminutive chased-silver twin-handled porringer.

During Victorian times, monogrammed hairbrushes, hair combs, hand mirrors, trays, and scent bottles were often arranged for morning and evening personal grooming. Revive this indulgence in your own home with a vintage mirror and your own collection of silver items.

Arrange the items on a lace-draped table or desk in good light for the morning and, as here, perhaps include soft candlelight for a night ritual. If you don't own one already, survey antique stores for a mirror that pivots on side posts with a magnifying mirror on the back side. A mirror with attached candelabrums would be considered quite a find.

Perhaps the most oft-collected silver items are salt, pepper, and spice shakers; they come in myriad sizes and shapes, as well as materials besides silver. They need not be relegated to display only, but can make practical as well as pretty ways to shake on everything from salt and pepper to cinnamon, ground chocolate, lavender sugar, and in the bath, bath salts and herb fusions for a candlelight soak.

p.s.
Fill a lovely shaker and tie on a ribbon bow to present as a house gift for a hostess or use as a centerpiece at teatime.

OPPOSITE
This elegant Victorian-inspired dressing table displays a silver collection of personal grooming items paired with an ornate mirror.

BELOW
These salt, pepper, and spice shakers arranged on a shelf make a charming still life.

A Passion for Lampshades

As is evident in previous sections, the Victorians were very attached to light and the way it was used in rooms. Recall the ways that draperies were used to filter light into rooms and offer a measure of privacy.

As you might expect, that concern for lighting extended to lamps as well. However, we may say that lamps were primarily a method of adding tantalizing decorative elements to a room. Clearly, the Victorians understood that a lamp could clearly illuminate and highlight the most remarkable artistic renderings. This focus on art was not limited to the shade, either. Equal attention was paid to the appearance of the base, how it worked with the shade, and where the entire ensemble was placed in a room.

The selection of a beautiful lamp can set a romantic mood in a room before it's even lit for the evening. Notice in these photographs how decorators and homeowners give their lamp collections special presence in each room. Taking their design cues from the details of the lamp bases and particulars of the shade, they enhance each lamp's impact with purposeful table placement and a concert of added embellishments.

It's fun to make the same lamp a totally different focal point from one vignette to another, using items employed to set a stage, so to speak. For example, the lamp with a dome-shaped shade, hand-painted rose motif, and a scrollwork metal base takes a more minimalist mood when it commands a tiny tabletop, just fitting within the confines of a marble square as shown at right. However, on the opposite page the same lamp takes on a more feminine mood with a rosy pink plate, a teacup and saucer with a floral pattern, and groupings of rose blossoms at the lamp's base. Instead of buying two lamps, you can make one do the work of two through different arrangements.

ABOVE

To repeat the scroll curves and balance the visual weight of the large shade, four round finials have been arranged as if they were feet to the lamp, on each corner of the little table. Simple, dramatic, and a terrific example of less is more.

OPPOSITE

A rosy pink plate, a teacup and saucer with a floral pattern, and groupings of rose blossoms at the base bring the garden indoors. The marble-topped rococo table and accompanying curved-back chair with a petit point center medallion of flowers repeats the cabbage-rose theme and the curving shapes of the floral lamp.

Art glass cast in delicate floral hues and intricate openwork "lace" was the height of Victorian fashion, particularly following the introduction of electrified lamps. When displaying a piece with so many elaborate details, keep complementary objects small to bask in the lamp's soft glow.

As stunning and impressive as these glass-shaded lamps are, Victorian tastes were not limited to painted glass alone. Why have limits when there are so many other materials with which to work? As with linens and shades, fabric presented a number of tantalizing embellishment options.

Fabric shades could provide a most interesting canvas. Most frequently, however, designs and motifs were stitched or glued onto fabric shades. Of course, the designs were frequently elaborate—seldom demure.

ABOVE
The cast-metal figure of a man enhances the drama of the openwork lace of the lamp and its tendril-motif base.

UPPER RIGHT
The framed scene set to one side repeats the rectangular wall panel centered behind the glass-shaded lamp. Such subtleties of detail delighted Victorians and please us today.

ABOVE
This lampshade has been covered with various lace doilies and trims. The glass lamp base is filled with white, cream, and ecru buttons, which are repeated on the lampshade.

Brocade Lamp

Victorians never would have settled for a plain old white lampshade, and neither should you. Of course, this project starts with a plain old white shade, but won't remain that way with your efforts. Adopt the attitude that lamps are for display as well as illumination and you'll never look at a simple shade the same way again.

Materials

- 1½"-wide wire-edged ribbons:
  dusty pink taffeta (5 yds)
  sage taffeta (3⅛ yds)
- 24"-tall lamp with brocade shade and gold base
- Fabric scissors
- Florist wires (16–18)
- Hot-glue gun/glue sticks
- Needle
- Pale green florist tape
- Sheer ribbons:
  ½"-wide pale pink/gold-edge (5¼ yds)
  ⅞"-wide pale pink/gold-edge chiffon (2 yds)
- Thread to match
- Wire cutters

Instructions

Note: For instructions on ribbonwork refer to Resource List on page 141.

1. Cut sage wire-edged ribbon into sixteen 3" lengths and twelve 4" lengths. Make each 3" length into a pointed petal leaf. Vary shape to create longer leaves with 4" lengths of ribbon.

2. Cut florist wire into twelve 5" lengths. Using florist tape and florist wires, wrap 4" leaves in clusters of three.

3. Cut dusty pink wire-edged ribbon into two 12" lengths, three 18" lengths, and two 24" lengths. Make each ribbon into a rose.

4. Cut remaining dusty pink ribbon into six 7" lengths. Make each ribbon into a twisted rosebud.

5. Measure circumference of lampshade at bottom. Triple the measurement. Cut ½"-wide pale pink/gold sheer ribbon to length. Gather-stitch down center of ribbon. Gather ribbon to fit base of lampshade. Repeat for top of lampshade as shown in photograph.

6. Hot-glue gun ribbon trims to lampshade.

7. Glue one 18" rose, two 24" roses, pointed leaves, and rosebuds to lampshade as shown in photo.

8. Cut florist wire into four 7" lengths.

9. Cut remaining sage green ribbon into four equal lengths for calyx shapes. Attach roses to stem wire. Finish underside of each rose with a calyx.

10. Wrap the roses and the leaf clusters together with florist tape.

11. Cut one 54" length from ⅞"-wide pale pink/gold-edge ribbon. Create one multiloop bow. Tie the bow to rose arrangement at lamp base. Fork-cut ribbon ends.

Victorians believed beauty in abundance was just about perfect. This spirited interpretation gave rise to the creation of a welcoming oasis in the corner of a sitting room. Decorative elements could be held in delightful cohesion by color, or by a combination of color and theme. In these spaces, the lamp was not always the focal point but did serve a central purpose in throwing light on the entire scene.

You could choose an elaborate spectacle of a lamp for a corner space and build other elements of color and style around it. Or you could use something more demure and simply have the lamp cast light onto a tender vignette, a treasured heirloom, or a vase filled with colorfully coordinated flowers.

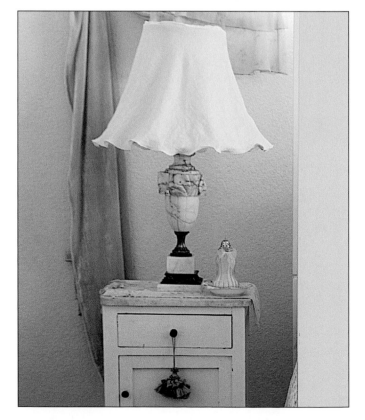

UPPER RIGHT
Notice how the paintings, pillows, prints, and candles—like the lamp fringe—celebrate tints and shades of red. A porcelain pitcher filled with red flowers further accents the tints of red in true Victorian fashion.

LOWER RIGHT
This lampshade has been covered with a slipcover to match the window treatments and bedding in this Victorian-style bedroom.

Tassel

Victorian tassels make an arresting textural statement when draped from or over a coordinated lampshade. A rather plain shade becomes decadent, perhaps even a bit naughty, with the inclusion of tassels.

Materials

- Bobble
- Variegated crochet thread
- Embellishments:
  beads
  cords
  tiny wooden finials
- Size 10 steel crochet hook
- Tassel

Instructions

Note: For additional instructions on crocheting, refer to Resource List on page 141.

For Crocheted Tassel Head: Single crochet directly over a tassel head. Start at the top of the tassel head and increase and decrease gauge to fit.

For Crocheted Spirals: Make a chain the length of the bobble, then crochet back into each lp of the ch three times to form a curly spiral. Single, double, or triple crochet back into the chain to embellish the tassel.

For Tassel Embellishments: Enhance with beads, diminutive silk flowers, cords, and tiny wooden finials painted gold.

p.s.
You need not use tassels on lamps only. Hang them from drawer pulls or other objects in a sitting, dining, or bedroom.

Victorian Clothing as Decorative Accents

The inherited clothing we treasure and the vintage garments we collect can all come out of storage to set a Victorian mood in imaginative ways. The following pages and the photographs feature interior treatments and vignette focal points in an array of rooms.

Hats and stick pins, jewelry, gloves, shoes, boots, button hooks, dresses and shirtwaists, gowns and hoops, children's and doll's clothing, and men's furnishings, all make exciting decorative details to incorporate into your favorite spaces. Gather a ribbon-trimmed hat; lace; porcelain containers to hold flowers, petals, or potpourri; and a statuette. Consider arranging your own charming personal appointments in similar ways, or determine what you want from thrift shops to express your passion for Victorian details as interior accents. Experiment with stacked books or recycled phone directories for the levels that suit the items you've chosen.

In many ways, the clothing display you choose for a particular room will set the mood for that space. Obviously, an elaborate woman's dress with embellishments creates a soft feminine environment. Cover with a drape of dark velvet, then with an overlay of lace before arranging the dress and accompanying embellishments. A man's tuxedo, with perhaps a hat, suggest darker, more masculine tones and accoutrements in a room. Play around with the feel created by clothing and see what you can accomplish.

OPPOSITE

This vintage dressmaker's form displays a Victorian dress embellished with lace, tucks, and tiny buttons. It commands the corner of this lady's bedroom and supports the cabbage rose theme on the bedding, the vase of blossoms, and many floral, lace, and other dainty details in harmonizing soft pastel tones.

ABOVE

Props from a bygone era and a child's christening dress make a fun vignette in a guest room.

The most optimal method for displaying a dress or suit is over a tailor's form of some kind, that fills out and animates the clothing. The next best choice is a simple decorative hanger.

Of course, any number of clothing items don't require added display expense. Shoes and gloves, in particular, can be placed or draped just about anywhere. You can put a pair of spats over a well-shined pair of men's shoes and place them in a corner. You might drape long dress gloves over the back of a chair.

Have only one shoe or glove? Don't discard that lone item. Instead, feature it with a few other vintage treasures on a bureau or nightstand. The accouterments for a travel vignette, for example, might include old passport books folded maps, journals, ticket stubs, postcards, and old photos in beautiful frames.

UPPER LEFT
These sensational high-top spectator pumps are the focal point of this arrangement; however, any items you find interesting could work as well.

ABOVE
Patterns of ruffles, lace, fabric prints, and trims are as delightful as a mural or a painting for recalling authentic Victorian details in a confined space.

RIGHT
This bureau features an assortment of carefully arranged vintage items that give the appearance as if they had been casually tossed here at the end of the day.

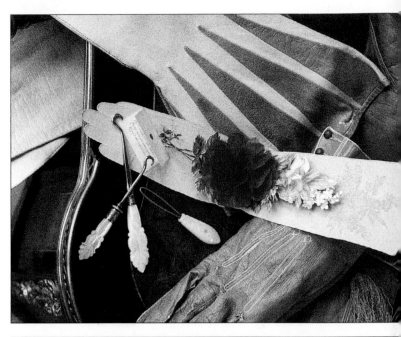

Closet doorknobs, for example, are just waiting to hold something special to set a nostalgic mood. Drawers need not be entirely closed all the time, and can protrude slightly to offer a glimpse into some other world.

If you prefer the cleanliness of drawers always closed, consider using the back of a chair or the arm of a sofa on which to display a glove, jacket, dress, or hat. An array of hats hung around a mirror makes for an interesting display. Using imagination becomes key as it is the ticket to getting those precious Victorian pieces of clothing out of the closet and into view.

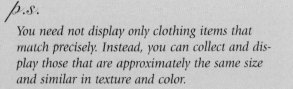

You need not display only clothing items that match precisely. Instead, you can collect and display those that are approximately the same size and similar in texture and color.

UPPER RIGHT

A partially open drawer, the cardboard forms that help kid gloves keep their shape, and a few scattered stitched-leather gloves make an appealing display with button hooks and a rose.

ABOVE

Children's garments on stuffed-satin hangers frame this Victorian bureau. Their paired symmetry is picked up in the pair of oval door embellishments and the bedroom lamp duo repeated in the mirror.

CHAPTER FIVE

A
Victorian
Christmas

Queen Victoria's consort, the Germanic Prince Albert, brought to London decorating traditions incorporating evergreen boughs, wreaths, and Christmas trees. No wonder Victorians claimed they invented Western traditions of elaborate Christmas decorating and celebrating with feasts, balls, and late-night suppers. The anticipated holiday season began weeks, if not months, in advance with splendid invitations to spend "the season" as a guest in London or at a manor house in the country.

A series of balls and intimate family events would be held with the expectation that invited friends and loved ones would have fashioned for themselves the requisite gowns, frock coats, wraps, and dancing slippers required to affirm the standing of the social circle.

In the meantime, host and hostess—not to mention servants—were emersed in the demanding details of decorating and food preparation for an army of guests. Sleeping rooms, the nursery, ballrooms, banquet halls, and drawing rooms had to be cleaned and groomed for the season's festivities. Special china was also reserved for use during the holiday season.

The planning and work required to create a smooth-running household was a staggering task for a Victorian family whose social obligations mounted according to class and financial means. Fancy embossed cards and invitations to holiday parties were carefully worded and used exquisite penmanship because they became mantel display pieces as well as calls to RSVP. One's social standing could be determined at a glance during a parlor visit by the array of engraved invitations in evidence, propped up casually but purposefully among the silver frames above the fireplace.

Country Victorian Christmas

As pointed out in earlier chapters, Victorian families enjoyed the outdoors, studies of plant life, and collecting. It is no surprise then that for country-style Christmas decorating and entertaining, they exploited the bounties of nature. In the first part of this chapter, the focus is a nature-inspired Christmas; greens and berries, pinecones, and folk-art items are celebrated. Though informal compared to Christmas celebrated in the grand manner as described at the end of the chapter, decorating for a country Victorian Christmas has no lack of delightful detail.

A country Victorian Christmas is lighter and brighter than its more formal counterpart. It is bright red instead of muted burgundy, a brightly decorated tree against a white wall rather than dark mahogany, and white frosted gingerbread as opposed to gleaming gold. It is more whimsy than pretense. Which style should you prefer? Why not do a room in each?

p.s.

When arranging candlesticks, don't fuss if the holders are of different patterns. Unite an odd-numbered grouping with a floral-patterned throw and gossamer ribbons.

OPPOSITE
This dollhouse under-the-tree decoration is typical of a Victorian country home. A sharp-sloping roof with symmetrical dormers and chimney stacks, gingerbread fretwork, and a broad veranda across the façade is made festive with a simple wreath and bow topper.

UPPER RIGHT
Candles need not be lit to be festive when tucked in a bowl among red apples and either natural or ornamental leaves or berries.

LOWER RIGHT
At night, a festive mood requires that candles be ablaze, and perhaps safely nestled amidst seasonal greens and ribbon.

Fruitful Nests

Imagine sitting down to start a festive holiday meal, and the first course presented is one of these charming little nests filled with fresh fruit. Now, imagine your anticipation about the second course!

Very easy to make, these evergreen nests are also ideal for decorating a tree, a window ledge, or a buffet table. Simply fill the center with artificial fruit, nuts, and/or berries.

Materials (for one nest)

- 10½"-long artificial leaf garland sprayed with gold or copper metallic paint *Note: Individual leaves on the garland should be no longer than ¾".*
- 11"-long fresh or artificial evergreen sprig
- Assorted citrus pieces
- Cupcake paper cups
- Custard dishes for shaping nest
- Green florist wire
- Hot-glue gun/glue sticks
- Maraschino cherries
- Wire cutters

Instructions

Note: If making nests to hold edible fruit, wash hands thoroughly, wear food handler's disposable gloves.

Wash, rinse, and dry evergreen sprigs on clean paper towels before proceeding. Keep gloves on to handle evergreens and carry out instructions.

1. Coil evergreen sprig into a nest shape to conform to custard dish size. Secure by interweaving and twisting florist wire to hold cup/nest shape.

2. Turn nest over and crisscross as necessary on bottom. Hot-glue. Allow to set.

3. Turn evergreen nest right side up and insert cupcake paper. Trim or fold as necessary to conceal edges beneath greens, allowing cupcake paper to act as liner for fruit in nest.

4. Embellish with leaf garland. Hot-glue as necessary at overlap.

5. When all parts are dry, fill with chilled fruit for serving or artificial fruit to use as decorative tree ornament.

p.s.

Create similar wreaths to go around candleholders. They can be used to illuminate each guest's place at the table, and might be included with place cards. Simply encircle glass candleholder with evergreen sprig, secure with florist wire, twisting to pull tight to the glass. Dot evergreen sprig and florist wire with hot glue to hold in place on outer surface of glass. Tuck berry and holly trims into evergreens. Add ribbon bow if desired. Insert votive candle.

Framed Print Arrangement

Think of this as a way of honoring Christmas. It is your personal shrine to the holiday season. On a mantel, buffet, or side table, create a country Christmas arrangement.

Materials

- Candlesticks varying in height (3)
- Evergreen trimmings
- Holiday greeting card or print
- Miniature topiary tree
- Photo frame
- Photo mat

Instructions

1. Frame the holiday greeting card or print. *Note: If using a photo frame that has glass, make certain to clean both sides of glass before inserting greeting card.*

2. Surround the base of the frame with evergreen trimmings.

3. Add three candles of varying heights on each side. Add a miniature topiary tree.

p.s.

Try framing several similar holiday greeting cards and arrange them on the wall by the front door for the holiday season.

An authentically Victorian country Christmas tree is ideally decorated with vintage or reproduction glass-bead garlands and adorable doll ornaments. Folk dolls can be fashioned from fabric, papier-mâché, or cut paper; just be certain to incorporate folk-art colors of red, purple, gold, and white with black accents.

And what of the most pressing question at Christmas—fresh or fake? Consider that the Victorians would not have had the option of artificial trees in their day, so it probably is up to you how authentic you want to go. Even if fake trees existed, with their focus on the natural world, you'd have to doubt that Victorians would choose to fake it during the holidays.

OPPOSITE
This Christmas tree is filled with replica ornaments of the Victorian era. The beauty of the tree is created from the large amount of colorful ornaments used.

UPPER LEFT & ABOVE
Notice how the red berries add a finishing nature detail to each pine branch tip. Strings of tiny red lights can create a similar effect.

p.s.

To create a Victorian-style Christmas tree, remember to use an abundance of decorations. It is less complicated to add more to achieve the desired style than to work with only a few items.

Baggy Santa Candy Ornament

Suspend this sweet Santa from a coat hook, doorknob, tree branch, or attach to a gift package as a trim. Place one in the center of each plate at a moderately formal dinner party. Give them out as Christmas gifts to the mailcarrier, the person who drives your kids to school, the hairdresser, or the pool person.

Materials

- 17" x 9" tulle, mesh, or organdy fabric
- Clay Santa head and neck, purchased
- Cord or ¼"-wide satin ribbon
- Cotton ball
- Craft glue
- Craft scissors
- Darning needle
- Pencil
- Photocopier
- Felt-tipped markers (optional)
- Red buttons (2)
- Red felt scrap
- Santa boots
- Sewing machine
- Thread to match
- Wrapped peppermint candy disks (4)

Instructions

1. Enlarge and photocopy Baggy Santa Candy Ornament Pattern on page 138. Cut out.

2. Fold netting in half lengthwise. Using pencil, trace pattern onto netting.

3. Cut out a Santa bag shape so that there is a front and back to his body.

4. On front of body, sew or glue on two red buttons. See photograph for placement. Turn buttons to inside of two body pieces.

5. Stitch or glue around edges, allowing neckline and ankles to remain open for insertion of head and boots. Trim body curves to within ¼" of seam.

6. Gather-stitch around neck and pant edges, leaving thread tails for gathering.

7. Turn right side out and insert clay Santa neck. Pull to tighten gathering threads. Knot, trim thread tails, and secure with craft glue to clay neck. Allow to dry. Let dry.

8. Cut triangle to desired size from red felt scrap for hat. Roll triangle of red felt into cone shape. Glue to secure. Allow to dry. When dry, glue to Santa head.

9. Fluff and glue cotton ball to the bottom of face for beard.

10. Pull gathers of both pant legs somewhat to form bag effect, inserting two wrapped candies in each leg as shown in photograph. Insert boot tops. Pull pant-leg gathering threads around each boot until tight. Knot and trim threads. Glue to boot tops. *Note: If desired, red felt scraps, ribbon, or cotton ball pieces can be glued as trim over stitching at boot tops and cap tip.*

11. At back neck of bag body, use darning needle threaded with cord or ribbon to create a loop of desired length for hanging from a knob or package.

p.s.

The Santa head and neck can be hand-molded from craft clay around a wine cork armature. With different head and feet, the candy ornament could become a doll, a wise man, or a Father Christmas ornament.

Angel Embellishments

Create beautiful angelic trims for packages, the Christmas tree, or place-card holders in Country craft style, using Christmas cards and cardstock.

Materials

- Cardstock triangles, width as desired in proportion to greeting card angel heads
- Craft glue
- Craft scissors
- Fabric scraps wide enough for angel gowns
  Note: Double if making place-card holders as "tube" gowns to fit over small bottles.
- Holiday cord or transparent nylon line
- Lace and rickrack trims
- Needle
- Small bottles or juice glasses for place-card holders (optional)
- Thread to match
- Victorian retro Christmas cards (2)
  Note: Paper doll children could also be used with wings cut from foil scraps.

Instructions

1. Cut angel faces and wings from Christmas cards.

2. Cut fabric scraps ½" wider than cardstock triangles. Gather-stitch with thread to create neck folds that fit top of triangle, allowing raw edges to fold to back of cardstock. Knot thread, stitch and glue as desired to secure gown top to cardstock at neck.

3. Glue greeting card angel heads and wings to neck of gathered gowns. Overlap onto gown to conceal attachment gathers.

4. Glue lace and rickrack trims to gown hem as desired. Fold side edges to back of cardstock triangle at base.

5. Create angel embellishments, using one of the following methods:

For Gift Embellishments: Glue to package as trim ornament.

For Ornaments: make a loop from a decorative holiday cord or transparent nylon line. Glue loop on back of each ornament.

For Place-card Holder: Omit cardstock triangle. Cut name card from cardstock and label with guest's name. Cut two angel heads and wings for each angel place-card holder. *Note: Cut one in reverse to match front and back.* Cut enough fabric to make a full skirt for angel gown that will fluff out and conceal bottle or glass support underneath. Glue name card to gown front, facing guest.

Trims

You know by now that the Victorians paid great attention to detail. What better time of year is there for detail than the holidays? Perhaps this is precisely when obsessing over details makes the most sense. Just think of the numerous ways in which details matter. Receiving a nicely wrapped gift is a wonderful thing. But a gift with coordinated paper and ribbon, and perhaps a decorative embellishment, is something else entirely. Should you open it or admire it? Little details will make a big difference in your holiday season. So, gather opulent trims to make your Victorian gift giving memorable.

What's Victorian isn't necessarily every holiday detail you employ. You can employ Victorian values in your decorating such as coordinating your family's gifts with the colors of the Christmas tree. Try decorative items on your dinner table that reflect the light from the chandelier. However, for items that are not as reflective as metal or glass, arrange them on a mirror or polished silver tray for a similar sparkling effect. By creating intimate, inspiring details in your gift giving, decorating, and hosting, you will help to create an inviting environment for all your family and friends.

ABOVE
This gift has been decorated with a variety of beautiful ribbons and fresh evergreen trimmings.

UPPER RIGHT
A paper-covered hatbox is the stage for beautifully wrapped gifts. The ribbons, artificial berries, flowers, and striped trims, all in Christmas reds and greens make this focal point sizzle with delightful details.

ABOVE
This holiday table features various silver hinged boxes that reflect the glow of candles.

Christmas in the Grand Manner

The celebration of Christmas in Victorian times was carried out to the extent of a family's financial means. In country house or city residence, the devotion to detail in decorating embraced all of the senses. The pungent fragrance of pine came not from the Christmas tree alone, but also from fresh evergreen wreaths and swags draped across mantelpieces and along stair banisters. Pinecones popped in fireplaces, which were kept from sparking on carpets by fire screens and leather-upholstered fenders. Added to the scent of pine were the aromas of puddings drenched with spiced rum and steaming brandy, and all manner of roasted game, fruit-filled pies and tarts, and walnut-laced stuffing. Mouth-watering tastes were only a high tea or next meal away.

The ruddy greens of holly boughs and their bright red berries accented green trees and wreaths as well as tall foyer vases and jugs on sideboards. Foyers and conservatories often boasted the trickling enticements of gently cascading water, while changing light streamed through a stained-glass window or flickered from candelabra or gas lamps. Some wall fountains had pockets and ledges for mosses and orchids. The glass-walled conservatories on the estates of the wealthy provided a bounty of lilies, orchids, roses, geraniums, and narcissus—all smelling as delicious as they were beautiful.

More gem colors appeared at table in the form of art-glass serving pieces, glittering goblets with gold edges and designs, polished silver, and crystal teardrops sparkling from chandeliers. Holiday clothing added to the colorful festivities that included exchanging sparkling greeting cards and prettily wrapped gifts. The opulent visual treats of Christmas were enhanced by the joyful sounds of the season.

Melodic strains of classical music and holiday carols were performed at private as well as public events. Modest chamber groups featured piano or harpsichord accompanied by stringed instruments such as harp, viola, cello, and violin. Later, gramophones, music boxes, and player pianos introduced a more technological approach to musical gatherings at home, especially popular during the Christmas social season. Guests were invited to perform with solo voice or instrument, or to recite appropriate poetry. It was considered de rigueur of courtship to be musically accomplished or skilled at declamation—the speaking arts.

Where country Victorian Christmas was innocent and bright, a truly grand Christmas was very nearly excessive, yet not quite. Still, one had to go all out to live up to one's social standing. The finest of everything was the order of the day, and guests were lavished with the greatest attention and the very best foodstuffs and libations.

p.s.

To emulate a Victorian-styled Christmas setting, group furniture and treat the tree as a tiered stage, beginning at the base with layers of gifts, or a Christmas village of miniature houses or perhaps a steam train.

OPPOSITE

This Christmas tree alight with candles is the focal point of this elegant Victorian drawing room. The tree decorations match the chair cushions and the rug on which it sits. Typical of high-style, the tree's decorations obscure the evergreens.

Posh Victorian Picnic Basket

For the ultimate in romantic gift giving at Christmas, decorate a purchased basket with lace, fabric, and ribbon roses. Fill it with wine, teas, coffees, cheeses, or chocolates for a special someone.

Materials

- 1"-wide ivory/peach crochet trim (3¼ yds)
- 1"-wide laces:
  cream (1½ yds)
  ivory (2 yds)
- 2" x 50" ivory crochet strip
- Doilies:
  large rectangular crochet
  small (4)
- Fray preventative
- Green satin fabric (¾ yd)
- Hot-glue gun/glue sticks
- Large crochet table runner
- Linen envelope
- Mat board, enough for basket bottom and lid
- Medium-sized picnic basket with hinged lid
- Polyester batting
- Ribbons:
  ¼"-wide black satin (2 yds)
  ⅜"-wide ivory satin (1 yd)
  ¾"-wide rose satin (1 yd)
  1"-wide dk. rose, velveteen (1½ yds)
  1"-wide gray (3 yds)
  1"-wide rose (2 yds)
- Rose velveteen fabric (2 yds)
- Satin scraps.
  beige
  peach
  rose
- Scissors
  craft
  fabric

- String of faux pearls
- Tablecloth with stitched floral design
- Tape measure
- White silk rosebud

Instructions

Note: Refer to Resource List on page 141 for reference on ribbonwork techniques used in this project.

1. Measure inside basket bottom and cut one piece of mat board to fit. Using craft scissors, trim edges so mat board fits easily inside basket. Measure basket lid and cut one mat board piece to fit. Subtract 1" from all edges of basket lid measurement and cut one more mat board piece to go inside lid.

2. Using fabric scissors, cut piece of velveteen to fit bottom mat board, adding 2" to all edges. Cut four pieces of batting, using mat board piece as pattern. Hot-glue batting to mat board. Center mat board, batting side down, on wrong side of velveteen. Wrap fabric around to back and glue. Set aside.

3. Measure horizontally from left side, down across basket bottom, and up right side for width. Measure vertically from back, down across basket bottom and up front for length. Cut one rectangle from velveteen to line inside of basket.

4. Hot-glue long raw edge of velveteen to top inside edge of basket back. Smooth velveteen along long sides of inner basket, gathering excess at corners. Hot-glue remaining raw edges to top inside edge of basket front.

5. Hot-glue velveteen-covered mat board to inside bottom of basket with raw edges down.

6. Measure around top edge of basket. Cut cream lace to fit. Hot-glue lace along top edge of basket and lining, covering raw edges of velveteen.

7. Measure around inside basket lid and cut 1"-wide gray ribbon to measurements. Hot-glue ribbon around inside edge of basket lid.

8. Cut piece of green satin to fit remaining lid mat board, adding 2" to all edges. Cut four pieces of batting, using mat board piece as pattern. Hot-glue batting to mat board. Center mat board, batting side down, on wrong side of satin. Wrap fabric to back and hot-glue.

9. Cut four 6" squares of rose velveteen. Fold each square in half diagonally to make four triangles. Fit one triangle to each corner of satin-covered mat board.

10. Cut 1"-wide rose ribbon into two 3" lengths. Fold each into V-shape. Hot-glue raw ends of each V-shape under velveteen corners.

11. Center satin-covered mat board on inside basket lid and hot-glue.

12. Measure around lid mat board. Cut length of 1"-wide rose ribbon to fit around mat board and hot-glue. Cut strip of ivory crochet trim to fit over rose ribbon. Apply fray preventative to edges. Hot-glue in place.

13. Cut center from large rectangular doily, leaving 1" border. Hot-glue inside ivory crochet trim.

14. Layer piece of rose velveteen and three doilies. Hot-glue to center of inside lid.

15. Make two 2"-wide rosettes from strips of green satin fabric, one 2"-wide rosette from ¾"-wide rose satin, one 2"-wide rosette from peach satin scrap, and one 1"-wide rosette from beige satin scrap. Make three rosebuds from strips of green satin fabric. Assemble rosettes and rosebuds into cluster. Hot-glue to center of stacked doilies on inside of lid.

STEP 15

16. Decorate outside of basket with remaining trim.

STEP 16

p.s.

Prepare small baskets or boxes ahead of time to fill with the remaining goodies at the close of the party. Use beautiful ribbons to decorate containers of yummies to send home with your guests as treat gifts.

ABOVE
This wooden container filled with Christmas candy has been decorated with a beautiful ribbon bow.

All aspects of Victorian taste were focused on Christmas decorating and entertaining in a grand manner. In this closing chapter of Victorian Details, we celebrate with level upon level of texture, glorious beauty, and romance. From intimate vignette arrangements of favored objects to entire rooms glistening with profusions of warm color, we can gather ideas for transforming our own homes to welcome the Christmas season.

Victorian Christmas in the grand manner was all about gold, silver, and burgundy. It was about precious gems, both for their value and their colors. And it was about light. There was, of course, the lights of the holidays on trees, in the fireplace, in the hands of joyous carolers. However, there was also the regular manipulation of light for added festive effect through the use of candles. The mixing and

matching of glass, silver, brass, and pewter candleholders, unified with only one color of candlestick makes a marvelous presentation. Our access to gold and silver candelabra is limited in the modern age, but candle choices are abundant. The creative use of these simple atmosphere enhancers lends a mood of festivity to any gathering. Try grouping candles with the tallest at center back and sides, filling in with pleasing levels for a symphony of light.

ABOVE
This table in the foyer, filled with blazing candlesticks and candelabra, is a dramatic way to greet guests. The blazing effect is doubled because they are arranged in front of a small framed mirror.

Sideboard Punch Bowl

This punch bowl, mascarading as a candelabrum, combines both gleaming silver and dancing candlelight to create an alluring table. Notice the symmetrical grouping of the candlesticks on either side of the punch bowl, and how the candlelight illuminates the painting leaning against the wall behind them. Finding something in your own home to use as background in this setting will greatly enhance the entire ensemble.

Materials

- 1¼"-wide wire-edged metallic gold ribbon
- Artificial fruit/flowers (optional)
- Craft scissors
- Dripless candles (8–12)
- Gold spray paint
- Punch bowl
- Styrofoam® balls (enough to fill punch bowl)
- White florist tape
- White florist wire

Instructions

Note: For safety's sake, douse flames when guests move on to other areas of the home. Never leave a burning candle unattended.

1. Spray-paint Styrofoam balls. Let dry.

2. Stack Styrofoam balls in the punch bowl and hold in place with a crisscrossed web of white florist tape. *Note: Artificial fruit and flowers if desired should be added at this stage.*

3. Insert dripless candle bouquets at different angles from each Styrofoam ball.

4. Make loose bows with long, casually crimped tails from the metallic gold ribbon. Fork-cut ribbon ends.

5. Secure bows with white florist wire in a flowing manner here and there among the candles by pushing the wire into the Styrofoam balls to camouflage florist-tape webbing.

6. Curve ribbon ends to tumble and trail over bowl edge at several points along the rim.

Appetizing Wreath of Cornucopias

I can think of no more fun and festive way to present nibbles as guests are arriving and milling about before dinner. These little horns of plenty will inspire conversation as well as give your guests a bit of sustenance. For presentation, use a silver tray as the base and fill the center with decorative accents.

Materials

- Beautiful papers such as gift wrap, marbleized paper, scrapbook paper, wallpaper
- Cloth or paper napkins
- Craft glue
- Craft scissors
- Hors d'oeuvres:
  dried fruits
  nuts
  pastry twists
  pretzels
- Paper clips

Instructions

1. Cut desired paper into half circles. Gently fold down flat side of each half circle and roll at an angle into cone that extends longer on the top than the bottom.

2. Glue and hold in cone position with paper clip until dry. Remove clip.

3. Arrange napkins in circle around tray. Fold as necessary so that one napkin can be lifted along with each cornucopia of snacks.

4. Stuff cones with hors d'oeuvre choices and arrange on top of napkins around tray with pointed ends toward tray edge.

p.s.

For a larger table and a greater number of guests, increase number of cornucopia circles as needed, but for each succeeding row added, place cone points in between previous cornucopias, as if they were petals on a flower.

Caroll's Posh Nog

Gratefully, the evening has been perfect. Your guests had a wonderful holiday meal, engaged in spirited conversation, and basked in the warm glow of friendship. How to conclude an ideal evening? Toast the Christmas season in high-Victorian manner. Fill your finest punch bowl to the brim with the most indulgent of frothy eggnogs.

Ingredients

Serves 50

- 12 eggs, separated
- 1 cup superfine baker's sugar
- 1 bag crushed ice
- 1 quart bourbon
- 1 pint cognac
- ¼ pint white rum
- ¼ pint apricot liqueur
- 1 quart whole milk, chilled
- 1 quart heavy cream, whipped
- Orange-flower water
- Assorted garnishes such as cinnamon, crushed cardamom, lavender buds, orange zest, nutmeg

Directions

1. Beat egg yolks until light.

2. Gradually beat in baker's sugar. Continue beating until thick and light in color.

3. Turn mixture into a chilled punch bowl set in crushed ice.

4. Stir in slowly bourbon, cognac, rum, and apricot liqueur into bowl. *Note: The quality of the liqueurs will definitely affect the flavor in the eggnog.*

5. Gently blend in milk and whipped cream.

6. Beat egg whites into stiff peaks. Fold into eggnog mixture.

7. Sprinkle eggnog with 2 TBSP orange-flower water.

8. Serve in 4 oz. punch cups and sprinkle each with garnishes to taste.

p.s.

Crystal saltcellars and their tiny spoons make a decidedly Victorian presentation of these condiment toppings, allowing each guest to indulge according to their preference.

Lacy Basket Ornament

Delightfully petite and delicate, this elegantly colored ornament is ideal as a favor for each at a formal table setting. As always, your guests will appreciate leaving your home with more than they had when they arrived.

Of course, just a few of these little gems will look great around your home during the holidays. Hang some on the tree or from light fixtures here and there.

Materials

- 3"–5"-diameter Styrofoam® hemisphere
- Craft glue
- Craft scissors
- Florist wire
- Hot-glue gun/glue sticks
- Metal spring clip
- Miniature artificial evergreen sprig
- Miniature artificial fruit
- Miniature ribbon bow
- Paper doily sprayed gold or silver
- Silver and metallic trims as desired
- Straight pins (optional)
- Trims:
  ivory or white lace
  ivory or white rickrack

Instructions

1. Using craft scissors, trim detailed sections of paper doily. Let dry. Using craft glue, glue doily to curved sides of Styrofoam hemisphere.

2. Form basket handle with a double-thick strand of florist wire. Secure by piercing ends into Styrofoam. Wrap handle with metallic trim and ribbon bow. Dot with hot glue to secure.

3. Coil evergreen sprig and hot-glue into place on flat surface of Styrofoam. Mound fruit and sprig, hot-gluing as you go to give illusion of basket full of fruit.

4. Hot-glue rickrack trim to basket edge and base. If desired, use straight pins at base to secure trim.

5. Hot-glue metal spring clip to base to create Christmas tree ornament option.

Ribbon Sachet Pattern

For use with Ribbon Sachet project on page 60

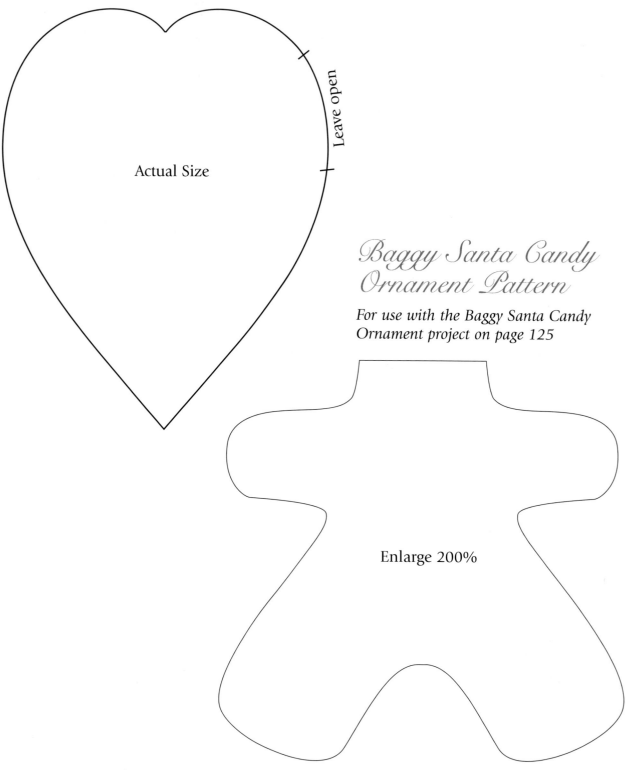

Actual Size

Leave open

Baggy Santa Candy Ornament Pattern

For use with the Baggy Santa Candy Ornament project on page 125

Enlarge 200%

About the Author

Caroll Louise Shreeve enjoys combining her twenty years of teaching experience in art and English into her writing career. She has published more than 250 magazine articles for adults and children. Her pen name for the children's market is Susie McGruder McGlish, her childhood nickname when "in trouble."

For adult nonfiction, she is the author/illustrator of *Life Is Good, a Guided Gratitude Journal*; and coauthor of *Celebrate Your Stories*. Her illustrations also appear in *Great Kids' Rooms* and *Creative Paper Doll Making*. Her in-house and contract editing experience for adult magazines and books for several publishers and packagers spans twenty years and includes art, bridal, business, cookbooks, craft, health, home, interior design, garden, scrapbooking, self-help, spiritual, style, and travel.

She is the former editor/designer of the *International Travel & Wine Association* monthly publication and traveled as a teaching editor for *Reader's Digest Magazine* Writer's Workshops team for ten years. Her first novel is being represented by her agent Deborah Warren of East West Agency in Santa Monica, California.

The mother of four children and grandmother of three, Caroll enjoys outdoor hikes and snowshoe treks as well as gardening and painting on site. Inside, she loves to scrapbook, sing, and transform her 1924 bungalow from "a ratty rental" into a welcoming, charming home. "My cottage is my canvas," she says. The faux fireplace project in this book is an example of her transformation acumen.

Caroll has been a writing consultant since the early '80s and has assisted many of her clients with self-publishing and placing books with publishers. Many clients have become dear friends. "I have a Victorian spirit about friendships," she says. "You just can't have too many good ones and I am truly wealthy with friends."

Resource List

The projects in this book may require reference material for the basic steps in some techniques. I encourage you to consult the library or Internet for such help. The following books may also prove informative and inspiring:

CROCHETING SCHOOL: A Complete Course
  by Sterling

FAUX FINISHING FOR THE FIRST TIME™
  by Rhonda Rainey

MOSAICS FOR THE FIRST TIME™
  by Reham Aarti Jacobsen

RIBBON AND PAINT EMBROIDERIES
  by Roslynn Haq

RIBBON FLOWERS TO BRIGHTEN YOUR HOME
  by Marinda Stewart

STENCILING FOR THE FIRST TIME™
  by Rebecca Carter

Dedication

For architects, landscape and interior designers, and homemakers everywhere who organize living spaces to warmly welcome eye and heart. Pass it on.

Acknowledgments

Gratefully, I acknowledge Jo Packham and Cindy Stoeckl for the delightful opportunity to research and write this book to accompany Chapelle, Ltd.'s Victorian photo collection. I thank my friends Marion Duckworth Smith and her husband Michael for her photos, taken in their stunning Victorian garden spaces in New York. Thanks also to Jodi Holmgren and Christine Pezel of Design Solutions in Ogden, Utah, for creating a beautiful layout design for this book that met my vision. A special thank-you to Krylon for supplying the paints used to help create the fireplace and to woodworkers Jerry Griggs and James Murphy for creating the fireplace featured in this book. Thanks to my family and friends who accepted the sacrifice of time together that freed my schedule to complete the research and writing of Victorian Details.

EDITORS
Leslie Farmer
Dave McFarland
Karmen Quinney

COPY EDITOR
Marilyn Goff

PHOTOGRAPHERS
Every effort has been made to credit all contributors. We apologize in advance for any unintentional omission and would be pleased to insert the appropriate acknowledgment in any subsequent edition.

Wanelle Fitch   51 (LR), 53 (LR), 55 (UR), 63
Hazen Photography   21–22, 49, 51, 61, 71, 80, 82, 88–89, 98 (UR), 99, 109, 130, 132 (LL) (UR)
Jessie Walker   29, 117
Marion Duckworth Smith   11, 16, 18–20, 24, 26–27, 29
Scot Zimmerman   2–3, 32, (L), 44–45 (R), 51, 79
Zac Williams   41
Reprinted by permission of Hearst Communications, Inc., ©2006. Photography by
Chuck Baker   91
Guy Bouchet   84
Pierre Chanteau   3
Gilles De Chabaneix   94

PHOTOGRAPHERS CONTINUED

Christopher Drake   43 (UR), 53 (UR), 54

Geoffrey Gross   86 (CR), 97, 127 (LR)

Gross & Daly   31, 32 (L), 56, 117

Yves Duronsoy   85

Joshua Greene   87

Scott Hawkins   104

Jim Hendrich   4–5, 12, 14–17, 72, 74

Jeff McNamara   62 (UL), 76 (L)

Steven Mark Needham   55 (LR),

Starr Ockenga   68, 116 (L), 127 (UR), 129

Toshi Otsuki   30, 32 (R,) 33, 35, 37–38,
   39 (LR), 46–47, 52, 55 (UL), 59, 62 (LL), 65 (R),
   66, 67 (LR), 69 (LR), 78, 79 (UR), 86 (LR),
   93 (C), 98 (LR) (UR), 101, 110 (LR), 111–112, 119,
   121, 124, 126–127, 133–135, 140

Luciana Pampalone   64 (L), 86 (UR), 114 (LR),
   115 (UR), 132

Steven Randazzo   13, 28, 93 (R), 108, 116–117, 144

Laura Resen   90 (R)(L)

Wendi Schneider   1, 43 (LR), 63, 67 (UR), 113,
   114 (UL)

Michael Skott   34–35, 42, 143

Joe Standort   36

William P. Steele   8, 69 (UR), 73, 75 (UR),
   76 (R), 77, 92, 93 (L), 95, 96 (UL) (LL), 100, 102,
   103 (UR) (LR), 106–107, 108 (UL)

Steve Tex   58, 114 (LL), 115 (LR)

Dominique Vorillon   110 (UR)

Metric Conversion Chart

mm-millimeters   cm-centimeters
inches to millimeters and centimeters

inches	mm	cm	inches	cm	inches	cm
⅛	3	0.3	9	22.9	30	76.2
¼	6	0.6	10	25.4	31	78.7
⅜	10	1.0	11	27.9	32	81.3
½	13	1.3	12	30.5	33	83.8
⅝	16	1.6	13	33.0	34	86.4
¾	19	1.9	14	35.6	35	88.9
⅞	22	2.2	15	38.1	36	91.4
1	25	2.5	16	40.6	37	94.0
1¼	32	3.2	17	43.2	38	96.5
1½	38	3.8	18	45.7	39	99.1
1¾	44	4.4	19	48.3	40	101.6
2	51	5.1	20	50.8	41	104.1
2½	64	6.4	21	53.3	42	106.7
3	76	7.6	22	55.9	43	109.2
3½	89	8.9	23	58.4	44	111.8
4	102	10.2	24	61.0	45	114.3
4½	114	11.4	25	63.5	46	116.8
5	127	12.7	26	66.0	47	119.4
6	152	15.2	27	68.6	48	121.9
7	178	17.8	28	71.1	49	124.5
8	203	20.3	29	73.7	50	127.0

Index